The Trump Movement

THE SECOND AMERICAN REVOLUTION

BY KEN JULIEN

Published by Julien Media
Email: kj@getmesometrump.com
Twitter: @getmesometrump

Dedication:

This book is dedicated to the six brave and patriotic members of the security team tasked with defending the people under attack at the American compound in Benghazi, Libya.

Author's note on the dedication:

I was in a "why bother" mood as I sat in a mountain cabin debating the effort required to write about the Trump movement. After all it was a lot of work, and I was an unknown author. I decided to take a break and see a movie. The movie I watched was - **13 HOURS: The Secret Solders of Benghazi**. After watching the movie, I was embarrassed by my hesitancy to put forth a very small effort to give back to the country that has given me so much. Inspired by the movie, I wrote this book.

Contents

The Trump Movement

Those who make peaceful revolution
impossible will make violent
revolution inevitable

John F. Kennedy

The Trump Movement is nothing less than the second coming of the American Revolution. I know, you are breaking out your sanity meters, but stay with me. Surprisingly, in the 200+ year history of our nation you can count on your fingers the number of seminal events that dramatically changed our future. I believe that the Trump Movement is one of these seminal events. The "Trump Movement" is a truly astonishing development in the history of our country. On the surface it may seem outrageous to compare the Trump Movement to the American Revolution. But below the surface, the similarities are striking.

Coincidentally, one the earliest, and the largest battles of the American Revolution was fought in New York City. The very same place New York born Donald Trump started his run for the presidency. George Washington's army barely avoided being annihilated by the most powerful military invasion the world had ever seen. Washington was almost undone by Loyalist spies among the population that aided the British. Likewise, Trump faced down the largest army of media elites, politicians, celebrities, and even foreign leaders to ever attack a political candidate. Like Washington, Trump was almost done in by the Loyalists (republicans) of his own party. Both lived to fight on. Interestingly, he will have won the primaries in all of the 13 original colonies by receiving a record number of votes.

People came to this land, which was not yet a country, for many reasons. Chief among these were freedom of religion, less interference in their daily lives by rulers and the ability to pursue a more prosperous life. The people that came here began to make tremendous progress toward these goals. Most importantly, they began to prosper economically through their ingenuity and hard work. When the rulers and elites of England became too controlling and greedy the colonies began the revolt. Trump is addressing many of the same issues that led the people of this land to revolt against rulers thousands of miles away in England. He rails against; rule by the elites, unfair trade policies, burdensome regulations and lack of honest representation for the people.

The colonists had slogans such as; don't tread on me, live free or die and no taxation without representation. Couldn't the Trump campaign use the same slogans against our current government? A government that that is working relentlessly to tax us, reduce our freedoms and to control every facet of our lives. A government run by elites with little regard for working citizens.

There is a good chance that the American Revolution would not have occurred without the oppressive trade practices of the English. Little remembered English laws such as the Molasses Act, the Sugar Act and the Stamp Act pushed the colonists over the edge into revolution. Hard as it may be to believe today, molasses played a key part in our history. It was used to make rum, which was a major, if not the most important, cornerstone of the early American economy. You'll have it trust me on this as it is too long a story for this book. In any case, it was the trade surrounding molasses that that helped spark the revolution.

One of the first key issues Trump focused on was unfair "free trade". He came out strongly against the NAFTA and TPP agreements that benefit the moneyed elites to the detriment of working Americans. Very similar to the trade benefiting the English as opposed to the colonists. Then, as today, it was all about who would profit the most from trade. You see, that's the funny thing about revolutions. You can slow cook away peoples' freedoms and rights, but don't mess with their money and livelihood. Trump zeroed in on this issue like a laser and it resonated with the voters.

Trump has said that it is not his movement, it is the peoples' movement. Not a huge number of people supported Trump early on. Not all the colonists supported the American Revolution. For various reasons many colonists were doing just fine under the rule of the English. These colonists were called the Royalists. Other colonists opposed the revolution because it would be disruptive, messy and violent. The thing about a movement is that it spreads faster and deeper than people can envision. As more and more voters heard the Trump message directly from him, out from under the cloud of dishonest media spin, the more they liked it. The more the people liked it, the more the honest politicians and media could come out from under the darkness and oppression of political correctness.

I believe Trump has given politicians cover to fight for the truth. His efforts will multiply as more public figures feel safe to fight for the truth without fear of being dishonestly smeared. He is giving ordinary Americans the courage to say what they believe is right. The courage to display a Trump sign on their lawns even though the signs or property may be vandalized by leftist thugs. The Trump movement is already exhibiting signs of accelerating. The establishment elites are now the ones running scared. Trump's courageous fight has turned the tables on them. Courage is the lifeblood that fuels revolution. The courage to fight for the truth is becoming contagious. And the truth will set us free!

It looks like it will be a Donald Trump vs. Hillary Clinton general election face-off. This assumes that the FBI or the polls don't catch up to Hillary before the democrat convention. As with most things in life, it doesn't hurt to be lucky. Trump may be lucky enough to run against what may be the most unlikeable, dishonest and corrupt politician ever to run for president. I know that sounds harsh, but that is what millions of people think, true or not.

If Hillary gets the nomination, I believe Trump will smoke her like a salmon. I think it will be the biggest margin of victory since Reagan beat Carter in a landslide 36 years ago. Why do I think this you ask? Because he will get way more black, Hispanic, democrat, union and women votes than anyone imagines. Why is this? Simply put - they are people too. They are not voting blocks of mindless special interests as they have been viewed by both parties. Trump treats voters like people, not like black marks on a ballot. They want the same things we all want. They want a chance to be the best they can be. They want to be part of something great.

Trump speaks directly to voters as people. He speaks their language in a clear and unfiltered way. He may be the most color blind candidate ever to run for president. No matter how the media and politicians try to smear him as racist or bigoted, the people are seeing right through these lies. He will speak to millions of people during his rallies. They will hear him, they will believe in him and they will vote for him.

This presidential cycle is unlike any our country has ever witnessed. Donald Trump has appeared out of nowhere as a beacon of hope, reaching out to guide our country back onto the path of greatness. He is uniquely qualified to usher in a change due to his wealth, accomplishments and force of personality. He doesn't need fame, money or power. He already has them. He is running to make America great, not to make himself great. He is running for president as a citizen not as a professional politician. He is giving hope and courage to the people that want to do better, to be better. He is standing up to the corruption virus that has infected our system. He is showing people that all is not lost. That we can in fact be great again. Trump is standing on the precipice of the biggest political upset ever seen in the history of our country, and perhaps the world. Strap in for a wild ride!

It's my Party, you can Cry if you Want to

"The men who crave power are best fitted to acquire it and least-fitted to exercise it"

Exodus: God and Kings

Donald Trump snatched the republican nomination from establishment elites like an eagle violently snatching a clueless trout from a tranquil mountain pond. They never really knew what hit them.

The Speaker of the House, Paul Ryan, appeared to be in shock after Trump swept Indiana to become the presumptive nominee of the party. He even refused to support his party's nominee. Image that, the most powerful man in the party, a man second in line to the presidency, in total denial as to what the voters just told him. He can only be viewed as small and selfish in light of his petty refusal to immediately recognize the will of the people. Ryan was joined by Mitt Romney and the Bush royal family in their refusal to support the party that had nominated and even elected some of them to the presidency of the country. Unbelievable, inconceivable and unprecedented. Mitt Romney, the previous nominee who all but handed Obama his second term in a humiliating loss. Or as Trump would say – "he choked like a dog". He viciously fought Trump tooth and nail and continues to do so to this day. Romney has truly redefined the term –

sore loser.

Romney, Ryan and others whine about Trump not being conservative enough. These two in particular have been all talk and no conservative action. Ryan just got done spearheading the Obama budget through the House without a whimper. Romney is best known as the grandfather of Obamacare. Many people claim Obamacare was modeled after the plan Romney designed when he was governor of Massachusetts. Trump has reminded the elites - it is not the conservative party in any case, it is the republican party.

I suspect Trump would have run as a third party candidate if he thought he could be elected in that manner. More and more people are choosing to identify themselves as Independent. They are sick and tired of being categorized as being mindless followers of the political class elites. The elites of both parties' revel in calling themselves "public servants". I want to throw up when I hear about the professional politicians' "lifetime of public service". The top elites of them have lived in unimaginable luxury on our tax dollars, and personally made millions of dollars from political connections. The Clinton "royal" family of politicians has made over $200 million dollars from their "lifetime of public service". And they are not alone. Meanwhile the standard of living for Americans is steadily declining. Exactly what service have they rendered to us? Maybe that is why Americans have been drawn to candidates like Trump, Sanders and other "outsiders". Can we just stop calling all career politicians public servants!

Donald Trump has shouted to the American people - you don't need a political class to rule over you! Many people are sick and tired of the Bushes and Clintons acting as if they are entitled to be president. Americans fought a revolution to throw off the yoke of rule by the King of England. Many would now claim we are being ruled by a faux royalty in the form of professional politicians. As the old saying goes - if you treat them like royalty they will treat you like subjects. Many Americans are revolting against this rule and they see Trump leading the revolt. What he has done is like someone throwing a fire bomb into the center of a medieval royal court. No wonder the professional politicians are scared.

Professional politicians of both parties are more alike than they are different. They seek to categorize and divide us in search of votes and money. They have redefined the phase - go along to get along. They changed it to - go along to get mine. They craft carefully worded speeches specifically written for a particular audience. They then read these speeches off of a teleprompter. Why do they do this? Could they be afraid that they may actually say what they believe if they spoke spontaneously? They seek to carefully control their responses to questions. Hillary Clinton has actually gone so far as to rope off reporters during one of her "meet the people" walks. The elites of the Democratic National Committee (DNC) have scheduled the democrat primary debates at times obviously designed to attract as few viewers as possible. Republican debates, with Trump center stage, are scheduled to attract as many viewers as possible. You can judge who wants people to hear what they have to say.

Trump speaks extemporaneously. He doesn't need speech writers or teleprompters to tell him what to say. He wants you hear what he thinks and believes. You may not like everything he says, but at least you know what he is thinking. He says things that may seem outrageous and extreme. I believe he often speaks in extremes in order to get attention. In a sense he is going big, rather than going home. He is opening a dialog on many issues that we have been afraid to discuss for fear of being labeled as evil human beings. The truth of what he believes hits you in the face like a tossed glass of cold water. Galileo said " All truths are easy to understand once they are discovered; the point is to discover them." With most politicians one would need to be a mind-reader to discover the truth of their beliefs. Do we really want to be ruled by politicians who hide their true beliefs for fear that we might discover them?

Jeb Bush has said that Donald Trump is not a republican. In many ways he is right. Donald Trump is an American first, as most of us are. I expect a HUGE number of democrats to vote for Trump in a general election because they also view themselves as Americans first. Over 40% of Americans identify themselves as Independents. For most of our history, America has been ruled by two political parties. One identified by a donkey, the other by an elephant. That just about sums it all up! More Americans are deciding they want out of the zoo.

Both parties have very passionate core members. republicans and democrats are faced with the challenge of keeping a large enough core of voters to win elections. It is hard to describe them without generalizing so please bear with me. Democrats have a propensity to accomplish this by handing out goodies like food stamps, disability benefits, free anything and everything. They have a very large core of voters who want no part of being "Independent" of these goodies. Democrats tend to vote 100% in line with their party on issues. Republicans have historically been non-democrats. Their herd is more fractured. As an example, in the 2016 Presidential primary the republicans had 17 candidates compared to just three for the democrats. Republicans have tended to give the goodies to businesses, but count on love of our country, religion or a strong military for many of their votes.

Trump is attempting to win the election by separating the less hard-core voters of both parties from their herd. He has chosen to run as a republican. It was a smart decision. In 1992 a candidate similar to Donald Trump ran for president as an Independent. His name was Ross Perot, he was a successful businessman and he was wealthy. Like Trump, his campaign was largely self-funded. Many, but not all, of his positions were similar to Trump's. He lost. Perot did get 18% of the popular vote, the most by a third-party candidate since Theodore Roosevelt in 1912. It is generally thought that Perot took more of these votes from the republicans. Bill Clinton was elected President over challenger George H.W. Bush. Many republicans blamed Perot for their loss in the election. Trump may be a lot of things but he is no fool. He knew his history and saw that winning the Presidency as a third-party candidate was an uphill battle, even if you were rich.

Trump had another reason to run as a republican. He surely analyzed the base constituencies of each party. The Democrat Party views itself as the party of the little guy. That may be but they are also known as the party of handouts. My purpose is not to judge their motives but simply to put context to their base voting patterns. In any case, a large number of people who vote democrat would not vote any other way regardless of the candidate. Many are living well without working and are not about to take the Food Stamps out of their own mouths. Who can blame them. Why would they vote for Trump? If I was making a good living off the government, I wouldn't vote for him either. To give you an idea about how many people we are talking about consider that over 46,000,000 people are receiving food stamp benefits alone. That is an increase of approximately 17,000,000 people since Obama took office eight years ago as the American "safety net" morphed into a lifestyle. Draw your own conclusions.

Trump's choice to run as a republican created obvious angst within the establishment elites of the Republican Party. The "elites" include a vast number of people and professions. They include vested elected officials such as the senior members of Congress. These senior elected officials have tremendous power to control their members. They hand out committee positions and raise contributions for less senior members. They base their hand-outs on loyalty (voting) for their positions. The Republican National Committee (RNC) bigwigs are part of this group. They enjoy enormous influence, financial rewards and power as a result of their employment. Campaign consultants and strategists, such as Karl Rove, are also included in this group. They also enjoy the same benefits. Lobbyists for republican issues depend on bending the elites' ears for their livelihood. So as you can clearly see, there is a lot at stake in maintaining the status quo.

Why are the elites so worried about Trump in particular? Quite simply, Trump is running his campaign his way, with his own money. If he does not need their money, he does not need to follow their advice. If he does not follow their advice, who needs them (the elites)? Certainly not the major donors who make large donations or pay the elites' generous salaries. Unsurprisingly the party elites waged an all-out war on his candidacy. They raised $200 million dollars and ran over 50,000 negative ads to try to beat him. They rallied their friends at Fox News and other sympathetic media outlets to trash him. They threw everything but the kitchen sinks at him. They would have thrown the sinks but they probably haven't been near one in years. They have "little people" to do the sink work.

The first line of attack on Trump was - Trump can never win. This phrase became almost a mantra by the republican elites. They followed a tried and true strategy of saying something over and over hoping people would eventually believe it to be true. I googled "Trump cannot win" and it showed 161,000,000 results. There is no question they got their message out. It failed. Trump turned out to be a different breed of cat. He doesn't back down. He gave interviews to almost anyone. The media wanted the interviews because they knew ratings would go up if Trump was involved. People got to hear Trump's message directly from his mouth. His popularity increased. There are still the few die-hards chanting the mantra that he cannot win but they are starting to look foolish.

So the elites tried other strategies to get rid of Trump. One of my favorites is - wait until the "grown-ups" get interested. As if all Trump supporters are children. Give me a break. Didn't work. How about - Trump has no experience. Nope, supporters are not buying it. They realize that the politicians with experience got us in this mess to begin with. Then they moved on to - Trump has a passionate base but it is small, his negatives are too high, he started fast but he has plateaued and he is not conservative enough. Sorry but these attacks didn't work. They drag out intellectuals like George Will who questions Trump's intelligence, then collects his check and goes home. Not so fast Georgie boy. Trump hits back. Harder than ever. Trump questions Will's intelligence right back. Trump does not act like a wounded animal that slinks off into the night at the slightest sign of danger. I'm sure many media pundits are absolutely dumbfounded by Donald Trump. They simply seem incapable of understanding that people are fed up with politics as usual.

Then there are the debates. What a great venue to cut The Donald down to size. The first Fox News debate was a doozy. The establishment sent out their crack team, led by Megyn Kelly, to put an end to this Trump nonsense. They angrily peppered him with questions designed to make him look bad. Ms.

Kelly even stooped so low as to play the "Woman Card" on Trump. They stayed as far away as possible from the issues that voters care about. They relentlessly favored establishment candidates such as Bush. They did all they could to take him down but alas it was not enough. Trump came out stronger than ever and Fox News came out looking like an establishment tool.

This is not only a republican issue. Democrat candidate Bernie Sanders has also branded himself as an outsider. My guess is that he would also run independent of that party if he thought he could win in that manner. Trump has often reminded people that it is the Democrat Party not the Democratic Party as the media likes to refer to them. His message is that the people of the Democrat Party are not represented equally. Democrats who are not affiliated with a special interest group such as unions or "disadvantaged" groups have not been equally served by the democrat establishment. If you are not attached to a special interest group but just a hard working democrat, you have been left behind. No wonder Sanders is attracting enormous support, much to the surprise of the establishment. The establishment's "anointed" candidate, Hillary Clinton, has struggled to gain her rightful nomination. Many democrat voters don't feel better off after years of rule by their party. The more they hear about the millions of dollars the Clintons have gotten from Wall Street and their Foundation, the less they like it. Sanders is awakening the democrat base to the duplicity of establishment candidates.

The bottom line is simply that democrats and republicans alike, along with Independents, are sick and tired of the corruption that permeates our political system. In fact, only about 55% of the voting age population actually voted in the last presidential election. These non-voters have been called the "lost voters". These lost voters may be part of what Trump calls his "noisy majority". No doubt many of these lost voters were so disgusted with the system that they didn't think it mattered if they voted or not. Candidates like Trump and Sanders could change that. Although Sanders is hardly a non-politician, he is being portrayed as one. In fact, there is polling by Reuters that suggest as many as one in ten people who cast a vote this year for president will do so for the first time in years, or for the first time ever.

Record numbers of voters turned out the first time Obama was elected. If you recall, a big part of his pitch was "hope and change". The number of voters declined for his reelection. Guess people just didn't feel the hope four years after electing just another professional politician.

I have no doubt most politicians are good people and have good intentions. I also believe most ladies of the night are good people as well. But they both do what they do to get what they need, or want. As Ronald Reagan once said "It has been said that politics is the second oldest profession, I have learned that it bears a striking resemblance to the first". There is no better way to describe our political system than corrupt. Politicians need money and votes to survive. To get the money, they must favor their donors. Trump doesn't need their money; he has his own. He doesn't need to be dishonest to acquire fame, power and money. He already has them. He is uniquely positioned to break the bonds of corruption that bind our political system. Trump will be free to do what is best for all Americans. The establishment can mock him, they can insult him, they can misrepresent him, they can do everything but control him.

It's the Jobs Stupid!

"President Bush has said that the economy is growing, that there are jobs out there. But you know, it's a long commute to China to get those jobs."

Tom Daschle

Bill Clinton surfed the phrase, "it's the economy stupid", all the way to the presidency. Trump has correctly identified jobs, as opposed to the economy, as the issue most troubling to Americans. The economy is doing ok, not good, just ok. The economy is being fueled by a flood of cheap money, engineered by the Federal Reserve, and given to Wall Street. The problem with that glorious flood of money is that Wall Street has turned it into a mountain of debt owed by us. Unfortunately, we don't have the good-paying jobs to pay back all this debt and to pay for the soaring cost of living.

Regardless of the phony inflation numbers made-up by the government, Americans know the cost of living is skyrocketing while wages are declining. Meanwhile our personal debt is being racked up in record amounts, just so that we can keep our heads above water. Everything from credit cards and auto loans to student debt.

The politicians have killed good jobs in this country for decades. We now have 92,000,000 people out of the workforce. Almost 6,000,000 people work part-time because they can't find a full-time job. Less people have full-time jobs today than did 10 years ago. The vast majority of new jobs today do not pay a living wage. We are becoming a nation of fast food workers and bartenders. An average salary today cannot support the same lifestyle we enjoyed 10 or 20 years ago. You have often heard this expressed as – Americans have not had a raise in 10 years.

So why have the politicians killed the jobs needed for Americans to live a decent lifestyle? The primary cause has been the political corruption funded by special interest groups that benefit from regulations, unfair trade, and foreign oil. As the Roman Historian Tacitus said 2000 years ago – "in a state where corruption abounds, laws must be very numerous". Trump will have to fight these politicians and special interest groups tooth and nail to get jobs for Americans. I do believe he has a good chance of succeeding for several reasons. His "America first" platform is giving him a mandate from the people, he is extraordinarily qualified to do it and the damage caused by the corruption has become unbearable for the American people.

Here is how Trump will actually allow and encourage our country to create jobs. Notice how I said allow? Politicians like Obama, Bernie and Hillary have never "created" a job in their lives. Sure, they may use your money to expand the number of government workers to further their own agenda. But a real, productive, private sector job? Get serious, never happens! In fact, they probably kill two private sector jobs for every government job they "create". Trump is talking about the ways he would allow our country to create good jobs. I would categorize them into four general categories; trade, regulations, infrastructure and energy independence.

Trump will revise our trade agreements so that we can sell to other countries as easily as they can sell to us. It really isn't as difficult as the "experts" on TV would have you believe. There are two components to fair trade. First, we require other countries to treat us like we treat them. Currently, other countries treat us like patsies. They know that we don't have the motivation or the spine to hold them to their side of the "fair trade" deals. Secondly, we require products imported into our country to be produced with some degree of compliance with our regulated norms (i.e., a company can't pollute a river as a result of producing products for us).

For the most part, jobs move to other countries because products cost less to make there. They cost less because people will work for less and more importantly, their governmental regulations are less costly to their businesses. I don't believe trade can be evaluated without considering the impact of regulations. In fact, I believe that the dirty little secret of special interest groups is exposed by our trade deals. Their dirty little secret being - it is more about the money than the cause. As an example, why do Obama and Hillary want to kill all coal related jobs while at the same time they encourage buying products from countries like China that burn coal to make the products? Just asking.

Our trade pacts, such as NAFTA, destroy jobs. We allow other countries to ship their products here virtually without restriction. Conversely, other countries tend to block the import of our products through tariffs and regulations that are intended to restrict imports. Hence, Trump calls our trade deals unfair. He knows a bad deal when he sees one. Hillary made a new proposed job-killing trade deal, TPP, a priority of her term as Secretary of State. If Trump is not elected, the politicians of both parties will approve this new job-killing deal in a New York minute! This trade deal could kill even more jobs than NAFTA. Truth be told, TPP would probably already be law, and killing jobs, if Trump hadn't exposed it during his speeches. It doesn't even take a genius to solve the unfair trade deals. It just takes someone to put the American people first.

Trump has built a business empire using his own money. He has created tens of thousands of real jobs. He gets how the millions of pages of governmental regulations kill jobs, and increase our cost of living by making everything more expensive. I have no doubt that he will relentlessly root out job killing regulations and send them to regulation heaven. Honestly, how hard could it be to take a hatchet to the millions and millions of pages of insane regulations foisted on the American people. I truly believe that we would be better off if we put a class full on kindergarteners with crayons in an airplane hangar full of these regulations, and then told them to have at it. Trump has already said he would repeal Obamacare, the mother of all job-killing and financially burdensome laws. It is almost criminal that Obamacare kills the very jobs required to pay for the doubling and tripling of medical expenses and insurance costs for working Americans. All we have lacked is a person with a mandate from the people, and the will to put ordinary Americans first to stop the regulation madness. Trump will bring in competent people, instead of political hacks, to begin the sanitization of our regulation nightmare and the bureaucracy that drives them.

Trump is a builder. He will rebuild our infrastructure and inner cities by redirecting our national resources that are being wasted, stolen by fraud and spent on nation-building overseas. Yes, we have had many large "infrastructure" spending bills passed before. Does the term "shovel-ready" ring any bells! Or should I say – make you laugh! Unfortunately, these bills were wasted on pork-barrel spending that accomplished very little except to line the pockets of the special interests. Could you even image what Trump could have done here with the $4,000,000,000,000 spent in the Middle East by politicians like Bush, Obama and Hillary? Trump would have spent it on improving our country. Trump will redirect our government spending beginning the day he takes office. He will rebuild our inner cities and infrastructure. And he will use American workers, equipment, materials and contractors. He will use Caterpillar, not Komatsu, tractors. His government would give out honest contracts to perform the work, costing a fraction of typical government contracts. Our cities, airports, roads, and hospitals will be, as Trump would say, beautiful! This effort alone will create millions of well-paying domestic jobs. And the result of the creation of these jobs will have a tremendous positive impact on the quality of life of our citizens. Trump has said that he wants our country to be energy independent. We import millions of barrels of oil from the Middle East when we have all the natural resources we need in our own country. We could create millions of jobs almost overnight if we would allow the production of more American oil and gas. They would be high paying jobs in an industry that is critical to our survival as a prosperous country. Production of our own lower-cost energy sources would also dramatically reduce our cost of living.

There is really no reason to import oil from the Middle East that is beneficial to the vast majority of Americans. There are benefits to various businesses and special interests. Oil and gas companies have a big investment in their non-domestic energy activities. Alternative energy special interests make billions from government support of programs that would be unnecessary if we switched to cheaper and cleaner domestic natural gas. And of course the politicians benefit from donations received from the alternative energy special interests that in turn receive the billions in government subsidies. Lastly, and more worrisome, there appears to be an effort to support the development of Iran as a nuclear power. You'll have to ask Obama why.

The jobs that would be created during a Trump presidency would accrue to the benefit of a broad array of Americans. They would be created in all parts of the country for people of all races. They would be union and non-union jobs. They would improve the lives, and lower the costs of living for many Americans. Oddly, it is the vast array of new jobs that will make it harder for establishment politicians to support Trump in his efforts. After all, the more Americans' lives improve, the less they need the politicians that claim to "fight for them". The new jobs created would greatly reduce our debt by allowing people to get off government sustenance programs and get productive taxpaying jobs.

Hillary and the Woman Card

"The Democrats have concocted this whole phony 'war on women' narrative simply to mask their dreadful record on the economy and jobs."

Wendy E. Long

Do we really want to elect a president based on their gender or the color of their skin? Isn't that what we have fought so hard to stop? The last two elections have proved that anyone can be elected president. We elected a black man with virtually no qualifications to be president. The result is, as Trump would say, our country is a mess. Not because Obama was black, but because he was not the right person for the job.

Now we have a woman candidate. Are we ready for a woman president? Absolutely! Can our country survive four years of the wrong woman president, Absolutely not! This is really a two-part question. Is Hillary the right woman for the job and is Trump the wrong man for the women of our country?

Let's talk about Trump and women first. It seems to me that the "woman card" was first dealt against Trump by Megyn Kelly during the Fox presidential debate when Ms. Kelly brought up his unkind comments about Rosie O'Donnell. Trump and Rosie O'Donnell have had a long-standing and well publicized feud. Rosie was a popular, outspoken co-host of the daytime TV show "The View". She Slammed Trump for not firing Tara Conner, Miss USA, for her substance abuse issues. Trump strongly fired back at Rosie. Trump responded "I've always been a believer in second chances. Tara is a good person. Tara has tried hard. Tara is going to be given a second chance.". They both used strong vulgar language during the ensuing feud. Megyn used this example to imply that Trump treated all woman like he had treated Rosie. To be fair, Megyn used Trump's own words during her attack on him. Trump later responded to Megyn's attack with strong words about Megyn.

So what should we make of all this? I think it is important to remember two things. First, Trump owned the Miss USA franchise and was not serving in elected office at the time. Secondly, Rosie was not averse to the use of mean-spirited and vulgar language. The best analogy I can come up with is a knife fight. It is as if two strong, successful women had pulled a knife on a strong, successful man and got cut in the process. If you get in a knife fight, expect to get cut in the process. But the Media has shouted - oh the horror of the man fighting back! To me, it has nothing to do with gender, it is simply life.

It is easy to lose sight of the big picture when we get caught up in the heat of the argument. I think this is exactly what has happened in the above case. Because of Megyn Kelly, it has been used to portray Trump as a woman hater when exactly the opposite actions were displayed by Trump. He did not treat

Miss USA like just a beautiful piece of meat. Trump did not just kick Miss USA, a woman, to the curb, he sent her to rehab. He believed in second chances and stood up for what he believed. He treated her like a valuable person and helped her to turn her life around. To me, this is a classic case of haters turning a good action into something evil just to advance their own selfish motives.

The New York Times recently published a report on Trump and his relationship with women. It was "above the fold", as they like to say, in order to get maximum reader exposure. Their 'star witness', used to prove how bad Trump treats women, had some interesting things to say after the piece was published. She said that reading the article was very upsetting. She was upset because the Times had assured her several times that it would not be a "hit piece" but that they spun her story to be negative. She also said that her story would come across honestly but that "it absolutely was not". She said "He never offended me in any way, he was very kind, thoughtful, generous, he was a gentleman." So there you have it. A powerful media newspaper, with unbelievably talented writers, printing it just about as wrong as you can, simply to smear a man they disagree with. If that is the best they can do, I'm starting to think maybe Trump is the model all-time champion of women!

Trump has had an extraordinary rich and full life. His activities have brought him into interactions with more people than I can imagine. Prior to running for president, he was not portrayed as being unfair to women or viewing them as unequal to men. If he were the woman hater the media portrays him as, where are the testimonies and lawsuits from the thousands of women he has had dealings with? They do not exist. On the other hand, there are countless examples of his kindness to women. I'll document just a very few of them and you can judge for yourself.

Trump put a woman in charge of constructing his signature skyscraper, Trump Tower. He did this over 30 years ago when women executives in construction were virtually non-existent. His organization pays women executives more than the men. He has supported Planned Parenthood. His daughter is the face of his organization even though he has sons. A former Miss Wisconsin spoke from the audience during a rally. She thanked Trump for his support of her and her "Mexican-American" son during her battle with an incurable disease. Among other things, Trump had taken the time to send her a hand-written note of encouragement as she lay in a hospital room, calling her the bravest woman I know. How about that for a woman-hater. I can't remember the last time I wrote a note like that to someone I barely knew, oh, that would be never. But then again, I'm busier than Trump.

Watch his rallies and you will see many women holding handmade signs. They say, Women for Trump, Hispanic Women for Trump, Black Women for Trump and various other women groups for Trump. They speak for themselves. I think it would be fair to say that Trump does appreciate attractive women and he has also been married more than once. Some in the media would have you believe that these are disqualifying characteristics for a president. I would take that in the context of - these are the same media members that fawn over the beauty of Hollywood celebrities. The bottom line is simply – one has to look hard to find examples to support the smear that Trump is a woman-hater. If you chose to believe that Trump has faked his treatment of women equally and compassionately during his 40-year career, I certainly won't change your mind, but maybe Lynne Patton will.

Lynne Patton is a black, female executive in the Trump organization who posted an unauthorized video on YouTube about the Trump family. It has since gone viral. She said she made the video because she said "I can no longer remain silent about the repeated and reprehensible attempts to align my boss and his family with racist hate-mongering groups, campaigns and messaging". At the risk of losing my man-card, I have to tell you that I was tearing up as I watched it. It was the most passionate and emotional defense of a family under attack I have ever seen. During the video she dispelled any notion that Trump is a racist, woman hating bigot as portrayed by the press and politicians. **If you do nothing else in your quest to understand Trump, the person, I urge you to watch this video, it will rock you.**

Trump has said that Hillary wouldn't get 5% of the vote if she weren't a woman. He has accused her of playing "the woman card". Hillary does talk about how much she would do for women. Her campaign does seem to be focused on her gender. Her supporters advance the narrative that - it is about time we have a women president. They rant and rave about "Trump's problem with women". They have even said there is a "special place in hell" for women who don't vote for Hillary. If the woman card was not in play we would not hear it talked about 24/7. It really is a valid question as to whether Trump or Hillary would be better for women. This issue needs to be discussed because it could end up being critical in determining who gets elected the next president of our country.

Before I continue with the balance of this chapter, I want to make one point. This book is not about Hillary. I really don't want to criticize Hillary but she is the one who decided to run for president and play the woman card. Besides, it is no fun because it is just too easy.

The question before the American people is – would Hillary be a competent president? If not, I don't give a darn whether she is a man, woman or Martian – I don't want her as my president. Unfortunately for Hillary, she has a long record we can draw upon to evaluate her. It's not a pretty picture. Bernie Sanders has said that Hillary Clinton is not qualified to be president. Trump calls her "crooked Hillary". The facts seem to back up both of these assertions.

Hillary appears to claim she is qualified simply because of the political positions she has held and the political activities she has been involved in. No one can argue that she isn't as experienced as almost any political figure in our recent history. Bernie has argued that she is not qualified because of her judgement, not because of the positions she has held. Even Hillary's supporters would have a difficult time filling a single paragraph with a list of her significant positive accomplishments in a 30+ year career. For the record, I don't count flying more miles, at our expense, then any person in history, as a presidential qualification accomplishment. The negative accomplishments as a result of her judgement are a different story.

I will use just the example of Hillary's actions with regard to Libya to give you an understanding of Hillary's judgement. The overthrow and murder of Moammar Gaddafi, the Libyan dictator, has been popularly called "Hillary's War". In her own words she said "we came, we saw, he died". It was to be one of the crowning achievements of her term as Secretary of State. She wanted it, she pushed for it and she got it. It was a bloody coalition military effort to "free Libya". Her personal style caused a very public dissent among the military coalition partners during the war. It takes a special person to cause military partners to publically argue during a conflict. But that is just a side story to the real damage she accomplished.

In short, she turned a relatively peaceful and stable country into a hell-hole. Libya is now a bloody, rogue, terrorist state. It is becoming a new hotbed for ISIS in addition to the other terrorist groups supported by Hillary during the overthrow. Countless thousands of Libyans have been murdered by the terrorists roaming the country since Hillary's war ended. We have also lost four of our citizens brutally murdered as a result of her actions.

You are all too well aware of the attack on our "diplomatic" compound in Benghazi, Libya while Hillary was Secretary of State. The attack killed four Americans including Ambassador Chris Stevens, whom Hillary referred to in an email as Chris Smith after his death. Stevens had been constantly begging his superior, Hillary, for more security as they were in danger of imminent attack. Obviously Hillary did not supply said security. Keep in mind that her boss, Obama, was in a tough reelection fight at the time. It is thought we only had people in Benghazi to put up a pretext that all was good after Hillary's War, and for one other chilling reason. The terrorists in Libya had possession of the Libyan weapons trove previously under control of their government. These weapons included surface-to-air missiles that could be used to bring down civilian jetliners. Our "diplomatic" compound was in reality an operating base used by the CIA to buy these missiles back.

So where was Hillary during the attack and what actions did she take to prevent their deaths after she put them in harm's way? Why did she falsely blame the attack on an irrelevant video? Who knows. She won't say. And what little she has said to us and congress has been contradicted in the emails she has been forced to release. What we do know is that it took the most powerful military in the world 13 hours to come to their aid. We have been told the military was ordered to "stand-down" during the attack. Hillary denies this. I don't think we will ever know if she ordered them to stand-down. But we do know our attack jets were only an hour away in Italy, while our vastly outnumbered and outgunned people were in a savage fight for their lives.

I refuse to try to get inside her mind to figure out why she engineered this overthrow in Libya the way she did. Why she refused to provide adequate security to those under her command, even when begged to do so. Why it took 13 hours to get help to those under attack. Why she lied to us and families of the deceased when she said it was because of a video. It would be too much brain damage for me to understand her reasoning but suffice it to say - it was extremely bad judgement about a lot of things over a long period of time. It's not like she just took a wrong turn on the interstate. Can you even imagine turning our entire country over to a person with this demonstrated judgement?

So, who would be better for women? First I have to admit that for the most part I don't even know what the hell Hillary is talking about when she screeches that she will fight for women. I'm not sure if she wants them to be treated equally or as a special class of disenfranchised people. Let's just cover a few obvious topics and you can judge for yourself:
-Hillary's billion-dollar slush fund err Foundation pays women less than men. Trump's companies pay women executives more than men.
-Hillary has been virtually mute on the rape crisis on our college campuses. At the same time, she was raking in millions of dollars for speeches to colleges.
-Hillary has not been very vocal, if at all, about Islamic Sharia law. At the same time her Foundation has taken in at least $100,000,000 from countries living under Sharia law. She has supported the importation of large numbers of Muslims, many of whom practice Sharia law. Under Sharia law, women are basically treated like dogs. They can be married at 9 years old, they can be beaten by their husbands, their clitoris should be cut off, they cannot testify on their behalf in court if raped, they cannot drive, and on and on. Trump wants to protect

us from radical Islam's penetration of America.

-Hillary unequivocally supports Planned Parenthood no matter if they allegedly rip out live babies and kill them for the sale of body parts. I'm not saying if they do or not, you would have to watch the readily available videos and decide for yourself. My point is that Hillary doesn't seem to care except to defend the organization, which is a large supporter and donor to her. Trump supports Planned Parenthood but not late-term surgical harvesting activities. Aren't half the baby parts that are sold female? Just asking.

-Hillary has been silent on the epidemic of violence and rapes by Muslim men in Europe while Trump has spoken out vocally against them.

-Hillary is supportive of very severe restrictions on gun ownership and the right to carry, when it is women who have the greatest need of guns for protection. Trump believes women should have the right to possess a gun to protect themselves.

-Hillary has had whole books written about her mistreatment of people and about her being unlikeable. Trump has had a few very, very, very well publicized runs-ins with strong women.

-This last one is difficult to write about since it is hard to know what is true with regard to Bill Clinton's numerous alleged physical assaults on women. One thing we do know, is that Bill Clinton had a relationship with an intern that would have gotten any male corporate executive fired and sued for sexual harassment. We also know that least two of Bill's alleged victims that came forward have had their lives ruined. Although there have been countless allegations that Hillary was in charge of the "hit squad" on the women that came forward, that is not the salient point. The point is that Hillary did not forcefully get to the bottom of the many alleged and one proven offense. At a minimum she stood by while they happened, worse case she justified the abuse or attacked the women who came forward. In either case, political expediency took preference over concern for women.

Tell me again how Hillary is going to fight for women?

Bernie and the Socialists

"The problem with socialism is that
you eventually run out of other
peoples' money"

Margaret Thatcher

Bernie Sanders sure seems like a nice guy. Kind of like your crazy old uncle. I think I'd like to have dinner with him. Who doesn't love the slogan "Feel the Bern"? The slogan alone is almost enough to make me want to vote for him. He is a refreshing politician, he says exactly what he means and never changes. I could see him being the ceremonial leader of a hippie commune had he not chosen politics as a more lucrative way to obtain power and make a living. Most democrats want to sneak up on the people about their plans to turn our country into a socialist system. Bernie just comes right out and says it - BANG! You have to respect sincerity when you see it, it is so rare in politicians.

It is actually terrifying, but not surprising, to me that so many people in our country support the concept of socialism. I believe Bernie could have run away with the democrat nomination if he had more aggressively pointed out how flawed a candidate Hillary was. Bernie did point out that Hillary is unqualified to be president. But he backed off when Hillary's media friends came to her defense. Being a socialist leader is not for the timid. Nonetheless, Bernie has attracted many millions of voters. Many of his supporters are students being "educated" (indoctrinated) at our colleges. It's no mystery why, since Bernie is promising free college for all. In keeping with the spirit of socialism, there is no plan as to how we are going to pay for free everything.

You really only need to have a few catalysts to spark and fuel the flame of socialism. You need a large group of demoralized people with a disregard for the rights of others. We certainly have that thanks to the corruption that plagues our financial and political system. You have seen a few of them in action as they attempt to stomp out free speech at our Universities, Trump rallies and even a few Hillary rallies. Then, you must have a large group of naive people, lacking knowledge of history. We can check this box as a result of the liberals' infection of our education system. Lastly, you need a leader with a match to ignite the flame. We have that leader in Bernie. Unfortunately for the cause, it doesn't appear that Bernie will get to the finish line.

Socialism has never worked in the history of the world. It has always resulted in misery for the masses and power for the socialist elites. In many cases it has resulted in the mass deaths of people on a scale rivaled only by the two world wars. I'll just give a few examples and then leave the subject of socialism to the next election.

Socialism's roots date back to the French Revolution of 1789. Shortly after the socialist mobs took control of France they began their programs of treating everyone equally. In one of their first actions the socialists rewrote the French penal code to say, "every person condemned to the death penalty shall have his head severed." All classes of people were now executed equally! Tens of thousands of "counter-revolutionaries" lost their heads to the guillotine. Before the revolution was over more than 1 in every 50 citizens had been arrested. Socialism was off to a great start.

Socialism kicked into high gear when Vladimir Lenin arrived on the scene in Russia around 1900. As many as 10-20 million people were killed by the state or died from starvation before it was all over. The state killed millions of people that disagreed with the socialists and anyone that the socialists thought might disagree with them. Millions more starved to death when the state took control of the farms. Crop production declined dramatically under state rules and regulations designed to increase production. Farmers stopping working so hard when all incentive to work was eliminated. But hey, they all starved equally.

Lenin was an amateur compared to the Chinese communist (socialist), Mao Zedong, who came to power in 1949. Mao himself estimated that as many as one-tenth of the 50,000,000 peasants would have to be eliminated to facilitate socialist agrarian reforms. Tens of millions of Chinese were murdered or starved to death during the communist reforms brought about by Mao. If you had, or been thought to have had, a different opinion than that of the government, you were murdered. China was a pitifully poor and dangerous place under Mao. Mao is famously known as the man who burned all the books. Kind of reminds me of our colleges where the socialists are eliminating all thought or speech that doesn't agree with theirs. No wonder students like Bernie.

Let's finish with two modern examples, Venezuela and Cuba. Hugo Chavez ushered in the golden era of socialism for Venezuela in 1999. We should be able to get this socialism thing right after hundreds of years, right? Err, no. Once a rich, prosperous nation, Venezuela is in a total meltdown. There is widespread looting in the streets, no food, no medicines for the sick, no jobs, electricity blackouts and inflation is running at around 700%. A hamburger costs $170, if you can get one. And my favorite as a sure sign Venezuela is now nearing the end of socialism, no toilet paper or underwear. As for Cuba, all you need to see are the relentless news stories of Cubans fleeing Cuba to get to our country at any cost, even their lives in many cases.

Socialism always ends the same way it starts. Violence and misery. Unfortunately, the young Bernie fans are no longer taught true history in our schools. And as the old Edmund Burke saying goes – "those who don't know history are doomed to repeat it".

The Black Puzzle

"Black people have been voting for
Democrats their whole life, and
they're still poor."

Charles Barkley

This is a chapter I wish I did not have to write. The smears of racism directed, openly or implied, at Trump require that I address the issue. I am ill-suited to pretend that I am qualified to address the issue. I have neither; personally suffered from racism, nor have I extensively studied the issue. I am simply offering one man's opinion. - A new thought occurred to me after I wrote this paragraph. Trump has done to me the same thing he has done to this country. He has forced me to talk about something I feel uncomfortable talking about. Interesting. Well here goes.

Never in the history of the world have so many of the most powerful people in world promised so much to a group of people, and yet, accomplished just the opposite. People with names like; Obama, Hillary Clinton, Pelosi and Reid have promised to improve the lives of ordinary black Americans. The lives of ordinary black Americans are worse now than before these people started "improving" them. Could it be that the politicians spend so little time with the people they claim to care about? Could it be that they spend too much time at black tie, big donor, fundraisers, playing golf and hob-nobbing with celebrities? I can't say. I can only see the results of their efforts, not their true intentions. Keep in mind, these are the same people that imply Trump is a racist and would be bad for black people.

I am not a black man. I can't speak to the black experience. From where I sit on an admittedly comfortable couch, I do not see a pretty picture. I am a product of the 70's when racial tensions were high and the inner city experience for white and black alike was not pleasant. I am now experiencing flashbacks as I watch riots on TV and read statistics about murder rates and joblessness spiking in our inner cities. There is true rage reflected in the Black Lives Matter movement. We didn't just suddenly get transported backwards by decades. Something caused this. One thing I know for certain is - Trump didn't have anything to do with causing this mess.

Black teen unemployment is reportedly almost 50%. In March of 2016 alone there were 45 murders and 271 shooting incidents in Obama's hometown of Chicago. Drug gangs are in control of many parts of the inner cities. Teachers are being attacked in their classrooms. Stores are fleeing many areas of the inner cities. In Flint, Michigan the citizens can't even get safe water to drink. Almost without exception, these large cities are controlled by democrat politicians, the very party that claims to champion black Americans. I'm not suggesting republicans would necessarily have done better. Rather, I'm suggesting that the state of black Americans can't be pinned on republicans. Every time I hear Hillary screech "I will fight for you" I want to shout – fight against who!

I believe the primary enemy of black Americans is corruption, not racism. Corruption has no color. Corruption is the enemy of all ordinary Americans. Race has become a big business. Millions of votes and billions of dollars flow to those who play the race card. Where there are votes and dollars, there is corruption. Unbelievable amounts of money have been throw at "improving" the lives of black Americans. Unfortunately, too much of it has been used to pay for the mansions, private jets, expensive dinners, and the extravagant lifestyles of politicians and special interest elites. Doubt me on this? The Clintons and Obamas came in to public office with a nominal net worth. It is now estimated that the Clintons are worth well over $200 million dollars and the Obamas are worth over $10 million dollars (and they haven't even left office yet when their real payday will start). Don't even get me started on highflying Al Sharpton and Jessie Jackson.

Trump has estimated the cost of our wars and nation building in the Middle East to be $4 trillion dollars. Much of this money was spent building; schools, hospitals, government buildings, water facilities, roads, power infrastructure, etc. in Muslim counties. Meanwhile our black communities are in disgraceful condition.

Some in the democrat camp have a propensity to shout 'racist!' at people that disagree with them. I have noticed that this is often done with no evidence to support the charge. I do believe that I can speak to that charge. I have not seen or read anything to suggest that Trump is a racist. I can see why some people might say that he is. I can see three reasons people might say Trump is a racist. First - most people are completely ignorant on the subject, they may have heard the charge of racism leveled against him and simply believed it at face value. Second – some people confuse his stance on citizenship status as being the equivalent of skin color or religion. I have never heard him equate immigration with race. Third - some people simply have a dark heart and don't care if it is true or not when they say it.

If Trump is a racist where are the people who were shouting it before he ran for president as a republican? You might as well be looking for the Holy Grail. They aren't there because he is not a racist. Where are the cold hard facts supporting the liberal media charges that he is a racist? Just not there. In fact, just the opposite is true. All one has to do is watch the YouTube video by Lynne Patton, a black female executive with the Trump organization. She paints a completely different picture than the media created racist portrait. There are many other positive testimonials regarding Trump and race. The most striking to me was one written by a high school classmate, that has known Trump for 50 years. His point was - that Trump didn't have a racist bone in his body during high school, it just wasn't in his nature.

Much has been made about Trump not forcefully denouncing David Duke of the KKK during a phone interview. Trump has said he had a bad earpiece and could not hear the questions clearly. Trump first addressed the David Duke issue over 20 years ago.

He has consistently disavowed what Duke stood for at that time and other times since. I think the frustration by the race industrialists is that Trump has not been strong enough in his denunciation. For the haters in the race industry, nothing short of the absolute personal destruction of people who disagree with them will suffice. They want elimination of free speech for those that don't agree with them. I don't believe Trump will ever get to the point of outlawing free speech, regardless of how distasteful he finds it. I certainly hope he doesn't simply to avoid false charges that he is a racist.

It's All About the Supremes

"A Bill of Rights that means what the
majority wants it to mean is
worthless."

Antonin Scalia

The nine justices of the Supreme Court are the last
barrier between your freedoms under the
Constitution and the politicians' actions. Possibly the
most important duty of a president, outside of war, is
the nomination of Supreme Court Justices.
Currently we have three justices that believe the
constitution should be the ultimate authority in
protecting our rights. We also have four justices that
have demonstrated that they believe the
Constitution represents just a piece of paper
containing suggestions that can be overridden by
current social desires. We have one justice who
can't seem to make up his mind. And we have one
vacancy.

We have a president that feels he has the power to
ignore the Constitution if it doesn't agree with him.
Obama has selected a nominee to fill the current
vacancy. All indications are that he would be a
rights-snatcher, giving the feel-good justices a
majority. Fortunately, the republican senate is
holding up the nomination until the next president.
We are truly standing on the precipice. The next

president will more than likely nominate three or four new justices. Those justices will decide if we jump into the abyss of a Constitution-less country.

The next appointed justice could give the government the legal right to take all that you earn and ring up unlimited debt. They have already taken away your right to see the doctor of your choice by upholding Obamacare. They have made "sorry we don't take Obamacare" a common phrase used by doctors. They have expropriated numerous rights from the states, such as local control of education, and turned them over to the federal government. They have taken away your right to pray in school. They may decide you can no longer hang a Christian symbol on the front of your home or own a gun. It may sound far-fetched but it is happening in many areas of our life. It may also sound good if you want guns taken away. Consider that it could also happen to freedoms you personally cherish. If they can take away your guns, they can take away your Iphones. Wouldn't be as much fun then.

Trump has released a list of 11 potential judges to be nominated if he is elected. The consensus seems to be that they will uphold the constitution in their rulings. This in turn, would uphold our rights under the constitution. This was also an unprecedented move by a potential president. It was a masterful stroke of genius on Trump's part. He accomplished two goals by issuing a list before the nomination. He provided a clear point of differentiation with his democrat opponent. He also put a sock in the mouth of the "conservative" never Trumpers that claimed he could not be trusted with justice nominations. Absolutely brilliant!

I cannot stress **strongly** enough – if the democrats appoint the next justices, America as we have known it is finished! You know, I have always said - just because something is popular does not make it right. At one time the democrat KKK constituency was popular. What if they had appointed justices that agreed with the KKK? Some mess we would be in now!

The Trump Rallies

"I do what I do. You like it, great. You don't, go listen to somebody else. I'm stickin' with the people who stuck with me."

Ice Cube

Almost everything you need to know about the Trump movement is reflected in his rallies. They are large, they are nationwide and they are serious. The media narrative projects people at his rallies as a scowling, disheveled, and violent mob of old white men. Really? That has not been my observation at the rallies I have attended or the dozens I have watched on the internet. I have met hundreds of people at Trump rallies and talked to many more that attended other rallies.

In order to get a clear understanding of Trump rallies you first need to forget everything you have heard from the media. They have demonstrated a negative bias toward Trump. Their ratings depend on dramatic video of violent scenes and out-of-context controversial statements by Trump. As an example, I attended the Las Vegas rally where Trump's "punch in the mouth" comment was made. I subsequently saw it, or heard it referred to hundreds of time on TV. When I heard the comment in person I took it, as my wife would say, as a throwaway comment. I didn't get the impression that it was meant literally. If you asked me for my top twenty takeaways from the event, that comment wouldn't have entered my mind.

The overriding theme of Trump rallies is quite simply – love of country. Trump speaks of America first, and that is exactly why his supporters attend his rallies. The crowds at his rallies are enthusiastic, upbeat, smiling, positive and friendly. The atmosphere resembles that of a rock concert. There are women, men, children, Caucasians and non-Caucasians all represented by large numbers. Some appeared prosperous, some not so much. Many are college graduates, many are not. The one thing they all have in common is that they love their country.

The size of his rallies are mindboggling. This is true wherever he goes. His appeal is not regional, it is nationwide. He draws over 20-30,000 at large venues and usually more than 10,000 people. As Trump has said, the media doesn't often report or film the size of his crowds. People wait in line for hours to clear security at the events. Some even arrive 5-8 hours early. Many times Trump has to start speaking while hundreds or thousands of people are still waiting to clear security. People that cannot obtain a seat will wait outside and listen to him over speakers. Before the election is over he will have spoken in person to millions of voters. No wonder the media is scared to death of him.

So what did people tell me. They loved that Trump ignored political correctness and said what he thought. They liked that he could not be bought by special interests. You could see the concern on their faces and feel the ache in their hearts when they talked about the lack of good jobs, not just for themselves, but primarily for their children and grandchildren. They felt "sold-out" by politicians, therefore they spoke negatively and vocally about the other candidates. They felt our political system is corrupt. They wanted entrance into our country controlled, and they **really** wanted a wall. They felt Trump was the only, and perhaps last hope, for our country. Interestingly, most of the conversation was positive with one big exception - politicians! They also disliked the efforts by "protesters" to rob Trump and themselves of their right to free speech. And they particularly liked that Trump would not let the haters shout him down. Most of all, they love our country.

You can also learn a lot about what the Trump movement represents by the behavior of its opposition. First and foremost, they oppose free speech, our most valuable right. They do whatever they can to stop Trump from talking and citizens from hearing. They have charged the speaking platform, they shout in the middle of his speeches, they try to block his entrance into events, they have bloodied his supporters, they have attacked the police, they have blocked highways and they have threatened riots. To date they have only succeeded once, in Obama's hometown of Chicago. Can you even imagine the non-stop outrage if a hater had tried to rush the stage and muscle past the Secret Service to get at Hillary during a speech? It happened to Trump and the media made the criminal a cult hero. The local police only charged him with a misdemeanor for the criminal federal felony offense caught on national TV.

I have an interesting personal story about a morning

rally I attended in Fountain Hills, Arizona. My wife kept telling me to go early since there were planned protests. I replied that since it was an early rally the protesters wouldn't crawl out of bed early enough to block my entrance. Sure enough, they did dangerously block the highway just before the rally. But they had gotten there so late, myself and 10,000+ people had already arrived! Too funny. There were also other takeaways from these protesters. One of the people arrested had been flown in from New Orleans to lead the highway blockage. Wonder who paid for that? The highway blockage could have been very serious had there been a medical emergency as Fountain Hills has only a few major access roads. They were only fined $100 and sentenced to 10 hours of community service!

The protesters at Trump rallies generally appear as an angry mob. This was certainly the case when Trump spoke at a hotel in California. This protest stuck me as particularly ironic. The front of the hotel was mobbed by protesters waving Mexican flags. American flags were grabbed from attendees, thrown on the ground, then stomped on and burned. They were charging the police, jumping on police cars and knocking down fence barriers. They were shouting obscenities. Hispanic children were shouting f- bombs while holding up their middle finger. Preprinted signs insulting Trump were held high. Trump has often made the point that the preprinted signs are indicative of a well-funded masterplan. Traffic was being blocked. Trump had to enter the hotel from the back of the building. Accompanied by the Secret Service, he had to cross a highway, cross a dirt field and climb through a hole in a fence. Please stop and take a moment to think about this, it is easier for many people to enter our country illegally than it is for a presidential candidate to enter a hotel for a speaking engagement. That just about says it all!

At a recent rally in Albuquerque, protesters even threw rocks at police horses. Wow! In my wildest dreams I cannot imagine a Trump supporter attacking animals to make their point. They also lit fires. By the way, none of the protesters that attacked the police and their horses were arrested including the ones in our country illegally. This is the result of the leftist Obama legacy. Let anyone into our country, hate on the police and encourage any action in support of leftist policies. This has almost nothing to do with Trump. It is all about getting what you want at any cost. Come on folks, is this the America we want, where radical leftists can even attack animals to get what they want?

I have seen many dozens of these protestors interviewed on TV. Their answers to media questions would be sad if they weren't so funny. It was like watching chimpanzees being asked why they liked bananas. Almost without exception they could not give a coherent reason as to why they were protesting. If I had to give them credit for a valid reason, it would be their comments that they want open borders and not a wall. We'll cover that answer in another chapter.

Nothing troubles me more about the protests than the silence. The deafening silence! The silence of republicans, the silence of the media and the silence of Hillary and Bernie as they watch angry mobs seek to prevent free speech in our country. Be worried folks, be very worried.

Make America Great Again

"Mr. Gorbachev, tear down this
wall!"

Ronald Reagan

To understand the Trump Phenomenon, you need to consider what Trump might mean by "Make America Great Again". I am old enough to remember when Ronald Reagan was elected President of the United States of America. Our country was the greatest country in the world but we were mired in gloom. We didn't act great, we didn't appear great and we certainly didn't feel great. American hostages were being held captive by Iran, jobs were scarce, inflation was rampant, oil was in short supply and the Soviets were rattling their nuclear weapons. Even so, we were great but didn't feel or act like it. Reagan's optimism, strength of character and talents put us back on the road to greatness. We felt united, not divided. Reagan's strength began the unraveling of the Soviet empire. He stood at the Berlin Wall and shouted at the Soviets – "tear down this wall". They did just that. The 52 American hostages held by Iran were released the day Reagan was inaugurated after 444 days of captivity. Our economy began to grow again.

Fast forward to today. America is still the greatest country on the planet. Unfortunately, we feel less great than we were or we could be. We feel the greatness slipping away. Donald Trump is a winner. He is a strong personality and he wants to make America great again. This has resonated with millions of American people. What might Trump mean by make American great again? And what are the world-wide implications?

I visited the BILL & MELINDA GATES foundation visitors center in Seattle recently. The foundation is perhaps the largest individual charitable effort ever undertaken. In bold capital letters it states - **EVERY PERSON DESERVES THE CHANCE TO LIVE A HEALTHY, PRODUCTIVE LIFE.** To me this phrase represents the basis of the American dream and its greatness. It does not say, every American, it states every person. It says, the chance, it does not say the guarantee. For many years the American system has provided the people at home and many around the world the best opportunity for that chance. In fact, the creation of this very foundation would not have been possible without American greatness.

No country in the history of the world has been "great" without a strong military and a strong economy. America has had both of these for over a century. Unfortunately, both are currently in decline. It is folly to believe lofty social goals can be achieved without either of these. In fact, without either of these we will be talking about how we can survive rather than how we can thrive. Even given the above, the true 'secret sauce' to American greatness is the collective positive attitude and moral compass driving us to do great things for the right reasons. I'll let you draw your own conclusions on where we stand in that regard.

History is replete with examples of great Western societies that resulted in human advancement. Examples range from Egypt 4,000 years ago to Babylon 3,000 years ago to Rome 2,000 years ago to the Incas 500 years ago to Great Britain a few centuries ago. They advanced science, communication, architecture, arts, medicine and many other disciplines. Unfortunately, they all had their flaws to varying degrees. All relied on military conquest. All relied on slavery. They were all economic and military superpowers. They all eventually declined. As they declined, their areas of influence fell into a dark period for a great many years.

When Rome declined the consequences for the Western world were traumatic. Western society went into more than a 1,000-year state of chaos. Vicious bands of people ranged freely, taking what they could through killing and plundering. Micro societies developed, banding together for protection. Advancement of science and the arts almost ceased. Large numbers of people died from starvation and disease. Human advancement came to a virtual standstill as survival became all consuming. The Pantheon, built by the Romans in 125 A.D., remained the largest concrete structure built in the world for over 1,000 years! Roads built by the Romans were still being used by people from England to the Middle East for over 1,000 years.

During the early to mid-20th century two world wars raged resulting in the deaths of tens of millions of people. No world power existed to prevent the rise of evil empires such as Nazi Germany and Imperial Japan. It was at this time our country became the world power we are today. Not unlike today, a large percentage of Americans did not want us to get involved militarily in other parts of the world. President Roosevelt had the will and strength to practically force us to support Britain in their fight against the Nazis. It was only after the Japanese attached Pearl Harbor that our people committed to ending the raging wars. I can't imagine what the world would be like today if the United States hadn't fought to end the madness. The world without a great society was not a nice place.

So how did we get to the position of being the most powerful country that the world had ever known? Upon the founding of America, a new great country began to emerge at home and on the world stage. The Declaration of Independence and the Constitution dared the American people to dream of a better country than had ever existed. Many of those dreams were attained. They accomplished great things. They have contributed to the advancement of science, architecture, law and countless other disciplines. Although it took too long, the scourge of slavery was wiped from our shores by a civil war at the cost of hundreds of thousands of human lives that were given for the cause. They put a man on the moon. They created unprecedented individual liberties for American citizens including freedom of speech and religion. They created the most generous and charitable country ever to grace the earth.

Americans fought and won world wars they neither started, nor wanted, to defeat the horrors of Nazi

Germany and Imperial Japan. They completely defeated nations in war, helped them rebuild then left them to govern themselves. No country in the history of the world had voluntarily left countries that they had defeated. Has America been perfect? Of course not. The Vietnam and Iraq wars are examples of that. Our intentions may have been noble but they were misguided. Generally, I think it is fair to say Americans have tried to do the right thing for the right reasons.

Today we have a President that apologizes for being American and actually bowed to the Saudi King. Our current administration seems to intentionally project weakness. For political reasons our military stood down for 13 hours as Americans were being attacked and killed in Benghazi. We have cleared the way for Iran to develop nuclear weapons while they shout death to America in their streets. We gave Iran about $150 billion which they are using to buy Russian weapons, European airliners, develop long-range missiles and spend on their terrorist activities. We thanked Iran for returning our sailors that they had captured and humiliated. Obama landed in Cuba on Air Force One to a humiliating welcome that did not include any significant Cuban leaders. China and Russia are buzzing our military ships and aircraft. Other nations no longer respect or fear us. When we are no longer respected or feared militarily our very survival as a nation is in jeopardy.

Unfortunately, it has become more popular for us to criticize our country than to contribute to it. We have become a nation of whinny spoiled children that throw a tantrum when we don't get everything we want. We have politicians that seek to fracture rather than unite us. We are losing hope, without which nothing good is possible. We have people who want to reduce civil liberties like religion, gun ownership and free speech. We have a movement to selectively enforce laws. An anger has built up that has propelled presidential candidates like Donald Trump and Bernie Sanders. Americans don't feel the greatness. Regardless of how disillusioned and mad people may be, we still have the strongest economy and military in the world.

Although our military is still the strongest in the world, just how strong it has been has varied over the past decades primarily due to economic reasons. Republicans have tended to build up our military. Democrats have tended to reduce our military, spending the money on social programs instead. We are currently embarked on an aggressive program of reducing military spending. Our Air Force is even scrounging in junk yards to find parts to keep our planes flying. If we ever reach the point where our military power is not at least the equal of any other nation it is game over. Financially our dollar would decline in value. It would buy less and our lifestyle would decline accordingly. The interest rate on our debt would soar. We would no longer be able to borrow unlimited amounts of money to fund our lifestyles. Many instances of nations suffering economically due to their currency declining have occurred during my lifetime.

Unfortunately, it seems to be in our human DNA to want what other people have. If we weren't strong militarily then other people would try to take what we have. A bully can always spot the weak kid in the schoolyard and take something from them. If America was not strong we would be the weak kid. If our dollar was worthless we would not have lunch money to hand over in order to prevent a beating from the bully. And there would be no world "bully" cop to protect us. In essence we would have no way to protect our safety.

Our country is $19 trillion dollars in debt. Each of the last two presidents have incurred more debt than all the presidents preceding them combined. Bush doubled the existing debt when he was elected and then Obama doubled it again. Sounds like a Ponzi scheme to me. In addition, we have no plan that will allow us to pay for programs such as Social Security without borrowing the money. Trump is correct, it is a mess. We are blindly speeding down the road to ruin. No amount of denial will change the reality of the financial situation we are in.

If we continue down our current financial path it is a question of when, not if, our way of life will be over. There will be no goodies to be handed out by politicians. There will be no secure retirement. There will be nothing to hand down to our children except debt. We will not be safe in our own homes. We will spend our time talking about the good old days. Trump is a businessman. He understands the concept of matching your spending with your income. He understands that both financial and military strength are critical for our survival. He feels that he is the leader to provide the real world experience and strength to make America great again. More importantly, he has the will and unapologetic desire to rekindle American greatness.

Not Skating on By

"Life's most persistent and urgent question is, 'What are you doing for others?'"

Martin Luther King, Jr.

Sometimes a person does something that simply deserves a separate chapter. Where a person made a decision to do something just because it was the right thing to do. Where a person didn't just carry on with their life and ignore an opportunity to help others. Didn't just keep skating on by. The summer of 1986 was just such a time. The Wollman Memorial Skating Rink renovation was just such an opportunity. Donald Trump didn't just keep skating.

The Wollman Ice-Rink in Central Park, New York City, had been mired in a failed government-led renovation for the past six years. They had spent over $13 million dollars during the six years and still had not been able to renovate an ice-skating rink! The project had originally been estimated to cost $9 million dollars and take two years to complete. New estimates to complete the renovations were at a cost of $2.5-$3 million dollars and were again estimated to take two years. The rink was a treasured part of Central Park. It had been utilized as a place people could go to have fun and relax. An oasis in the midst of the concrete jungle of the big city. A place were families could shrug off the stresses of everyday life. All at an affordable price. But alas, it laid unused.

It was then that Trump stopped skating and wrote a letter to the Mayor of New York City, Mr. Koch. In the letter Trump offered to finish the rink by the end of the year. In the letter he stated that he had built Trump Tower in 26 months and that he saw no reason the rink couldn't be completed in four months. He also offered to operate the rink and turn over any profits to charities. The City had expected the rink to generate losses as opposed to profits. Trump disagreed. After intense negotiations between Trump and the Mayor, an agreement was reached where Trump would complete the project and manage the rink.

In November of 1986 the beautifully renovated Wollman Memorial Rink reopened! It was completed at a cost that was $750,000 under budget and ahead of schedule. In April of 1987 it was reported that the rink netted a profit of $400,000-$500,000. The City had expected significant losses to be incurred operating the Rink. A record number of 225,000 people were able to enjoy the rink at an affordable cost of $4.50 during its first season. And it was beautiful!

As of April, 1987 money from the profits of that first season had been allocated as follows:
$25,000 for the Partnership for the Homeless
$25,000 for United Cerebral Palsy
$25,000 for the Gay Men's Health Crisis
$75,000 to renovate a playground in each
        of the 5 boroughs of the city
More donations to various charities were to follow. All of this because one man wanted people to have a skating rink.

Drowning in Debt

"People need to believe they can
make a difference - that one person
standing strong can turn the tide."

Ann Aguirre

If you have ever sat on a beach you have surely
marveled at the relentless procession of waves
lapping at the sand. Minute after minute, hour after
hour, day after day, year after year the waves
relentlessly, endlessly, keep rolling in. Picture in
your mind a bottle riding upon each of these waves.
Inside each bottle is an unpaid bill with your name
on it. You stuff these bills in your pockets. Then you
need more room so you stuff them in your
backpack. Then you need still more room so your fill
your cooler with bills. You still run out of room but
the never-ending waves keep coming. You realize
there is no way you could ever pay all of these bills.
You look down the beach and everyone is collecting
their own bottles.

Eventually you need to rest while the bottles pile up
at your feet. You pick a bill out of your pocket and
examine it. Suddenly you realize that you didn't buy
this stuff. When you look down the beach everyone
is yelling "hey I didn't buy this crap". You are
becoming angry and confused so you look closer at
a bill. You notice in the small print that it says that

your parents or someone else signed your name for their purchase. Everyone is now screaming "my parents didn't get my permission to put me into endless debt"! An accountant on the beach has estimated the amount of all the bills scooped up by everyone so far to be almost $60,000 for every adult and child on the beach. And yet they keep coming. All you wanted was a nice picnic at the beach!

The bottles on the waves were imaginary, but the $60,000 in debt for every man, woman and child in American is real. Over $19 trillion in total as a country. Yet the bad news keeps coming. This amount is only for our federal debt, we haven't even taken into account state and local government debt. Just unpaid bills for state government employee pensions alone are estimated to come in at over $4,000 per person. And this amount doesn't count an estimated $80-$100 trillions of future bills for promises such as Social Security and Medicare. Isn't everyone sick and tired of adjusting their own purchases as things cost more and real wages decline? Then why do we allow the politicians to spend without limits?

So how did we get in this mess if we didn't personally sign for all these debts? We voted for them, that's how. Every time we voted for an elected official we either directly or indirectly authorized them to spend our tax money as they please and run up debts on our behalf. You could also have chosen not to vote and let other people select on your behalf. Those votes also allow elected officials to decide many other things for you. You authorized them to decide what freedoms you can keep. They decide if you can worship as you want, if you can have a gun, which doctor you can see, what you can say publicly, who can enter the country, if we should have safe streets, how you should be protected from terrorists and an endless list of other matters. Still think it doesn't matter which candidate you vote for?

There are estimated to be over 500,000 elected officials in this country. These officials manage millions of employees. All of these people are making decisions, small or large, on our behalf. I can hear it now; I didn't want them to have all this power. Not to worry, they have thousands of lobbyists to help them make the right choices for you. Unfortunately, not many of us has a lobbyist working on our behalf. There is also the Constitution of the United States to put a limit on what they can do. But popular culture is drifting toward an attitude of interpreting the Constitution as an old outdated piece of paper not to be taken too seriously.

It is not only public debt that is being piled up. Take the case of the Teamsters pension fund representing more than 400,000 members. The fund has about $20 billion of future obligations to retirees that it will not be able to pay. The fund takes in $1 a day for every $3 it pays out which adds $2 billion a year to their deficit. These retirees are going to see as much as a 50% reduction in their pension payments. That is going to sting. Although this is a private plan, it is overseen by the government (for the protection of the workers). Of course the overseers have entrusted the funds to their wall street friends. Now it is a mess.

As I write this, our government and their wall street

friends are scheming to bail-out $70 billion of Puerto Rican debt. Any guesses who will win and who will lose on this deal? On and on the debt waves roll in.

Let's be crystal clear about one thing. There is no happy ending to the debt story. The only ways out are rampant inflation or bankruptcy. Either choice would result in Americans living like the citizens of a third-world country. We are adding to our debt each and every day by spending more than we make. We are expanding our funding requirements every time someone crosses our borders and is provided a comfortable work-free life. We are adding to our debt spiral every time a politician gives out free anything with money we don't have to give. We are blissfully "getting ours" while we selfie our way to serfdom.

But there is hope that we can stem the tide of debt. As long as we maintain the strongest economy in the world we can support the debt we have. We just need to stop adding to it. Here is where a businessperson like Trump can help. He has spent his whole life operating under the principle that a business can't incur endless amounts of debt with no possible ability to repay them. We simply cannot continue to pile on the debt and expect that dire consequences will not follow. Calling people who tell the truth about our spending and debt negative and mean-spirited will not stem one wave of the tide. Trump is not afraid to tell the truth.

Why are Americans Angry?

"I'm as mad as hell, and I'm not going
to take this anymore."

NETWORK

Of course Americans are angry, so is Trump. He says that he is angry over the incompetence of our leaders. Trump is saying that he is angry over what is happening to our country. Try to find someone who isn't. You can't turn on TV "news" or commentary programs without people shouting at one another. People are called racist, bigots, religious extremists, right wing or left wing simply because they have a different opinion. I guess it is easier just to insult people than to defend your opinion with facts. Even the President can't seem to make a public speech of any kind without looking angry and insulting people who disagree with him. Where is the laughter?

In 1976 a popular motion picture titled "Network" was released. The movie starred Peter Finch as a network anchor. He was the first actor to win a posthumous Academy Award for Best Actor in a leading role for his performance. In the film, Finch had a meltdown while live on air. Finch went into a tirade about the problems ordinary people faced and the hopelessness they felt in dealing with the problems. He then shouted the now memorable words "I'M AS MAD AS HELL, AND I'M NOT

GOING TO TAKE THIS ANYMORE!". He then urged everyone watching his broadcast to get up and shout these words out their windows. They then cut to show people all around the country opening windows and shouting this phrase. Nothing explains the Trump phenomenon better than the scene from this film. Some of the issues have changed but most of them are the same. Finch shouted of crime, inflation, loss of or fear of losing a job, the environment and other current events. Consider that the film aired in 1977. That is almost 40 years ago and things have only gotten worse. No wonder people are mad.

The Republican elites dragged out South Carolina Republican Governor Nikki Haley to give the rebuttal to the 2016 Democrat State of the Union political address. She felt that we needed to ignore "the siren call of the angriest voices". The specific issue Ms. Haley brought up seemed to take issue with Trump's opposition to illegal immigration. She went on to say no one willing to work hard should feel unwelcome in this country. Many American are angry with the damage illegal immigration has done to our country. She is telling us that we have no right to be angry. Keep in mind that she was handpicked by Republican rulers to deliver this message. Her message was a thinly disguised attack on the Trump movement. Ok, so let's unpack this. This was not only an attack on Donald Trump but by association his supporters as well. Why would they attack their leading candidate in the Republican presidential primary and the millions of Americans who support him? Could it be that they are scared of someone upsetting their applecart? It makes you wonder if they would rather lose the election than get bumped from their spot at the pork trough. After all the current elites are feeding pretty well at the public trough. Really Ms. Haley, are we supposed to sit down and shut up while the political elites run this country into the ground? Do the elites think we are stupid?

What are the things Trump is saying we are angry about? Often he frames things in terms of winning and losing. There is an old saying - if you are not winning then you are losing. If you are losing, you are feeling a loss of hope and a sense of powerlessness. Why are we feeling less hopeful and more powerless? It is because we are feeling that we have lost control of the events affecting our daily lives. It is no accident that Obama won the last two elections on the message of hope and change. We got the change but obviously we're not feeling the hope eight years later. In January of 2016 a single power ball lottery reached 1.5 billion dollars. The amount of tickets bought is a perfect visualization of our thirst(hope) for a better life.

In order to define a solution to a problem you would first need to define the problem. Trump has spent considerable time to define the problems. Trump can appear negative by constantly identifying the problems. Unfortunately, unless he does identify the problems he cannot effectively outline his solutions. A book, like a campaign should lay out the problems before the solutions. As I write out the problems it makes me want to jump out of the window rather than shout out of it. Anyway here goes.

First and foremost, our standard of living is declining. We are losing the financial battle in our daily lives. Wages are falling far short of the amount needed to live a decent life. Meanwhile our costs of living are skyrocketing. We see the people on Wall Street and in Washington D.C. living large while we are living small. Taxes are out of control. Everything including income taxes, property taxes, sales taxes, use fees and now even hundreds of health care taxes from Obamacare. Everything seems to cost more including rents, cars, food, and most of all health care. People feel that if they work hard and play by the rules that they are being screwed.

Most of the increase in the cost of living has been loaded on us by the government and Wall Street. The government imposes thousands of regulations and taxes on our economy that end up costing us more. Health care is a perfect example. Insurance premiums and deductibles have skyrocketed as a direct result of Obamacare. Wall Street and the Federal Reserve create asset bubbles designed to enrich themselves at our expense. Interest rates have been driven to zero by the Federal Reserve. With zero interest rates, seniors cannot earn enough interest to support themselves. Rental housing is another example. Rents have been steadily increasing to the point of not being affordable for many Americans. Great for the landlords, not so much for the renters.

Trump hits hard on what are called "Free Trade" agreements signed by our professional politicians. Americans look around and see shuttered factories. They don't see living wage jobs. Fair Trade is code for the Clinton-Bush policy of cheap labor for business. They have entered into trade agreements that Trump feels have transferred millions of good jobs to other countries. Both parties receive untold millions of political campaign dollars from big businesses that employ thousands of lobbyists. Understandably their lobbyists do not seem to have jobs, except theirs, as a high priority. I don't know about you but I don't employ a lobbyist. Our politicians pay attention to what their donors' lobbyists tell them. Therefore, as Trump says, we lose in all these agreements. He wants to win and as a result create jobs for you and I.

Trump spends a lot of time talking about our veterans. They have been under served by our government run health care system established for them. Thousands and thousands of them are homeless. You cannot drive in our cities without seeing the scores of homeless, many of whom are veterans. It has been estimated that 22 veterans commit suicide every day. Our government choses to spend our money in other ways. For instance, on people who enter the country illegally. We provide health care, feed, house and educate everyone who chooses to enter our country illegally. Even more appalling our President is bringing in thousands of "refugees", that may include terrorists, with the same fully paid great lifestyle. Yet our veterans, who make this country free, go without adequate health care and in many cases without a place to live. Trump is angry about this treatment of our veterans.

Americans are fearful about terrorism. They should be. We have had dozens and dozens of attacks in our country since 9/11. Most were not identified as terrorism by our government. Events such as shootings of police officers, be-headings in the Midwest, a shooting at Fort Hood, a bombing at the

Boston Marathon, stabbings at a community college, most covered up as non-terrorist acts such as workplace violence or the work of unaligned "lone-wolves". Try as they may the government cannot hide the scourge of Radical Islamic Terrorism that has descended upon our land. Trump has proposed steps to prevent terrorism yet our government seems to choose political correctness over our safety. Trump has spoken out as being for our safety first.

Virtually every week a police officer is murdered on our streets. Is it just me or does it seem as if criminals are more valued than our police officers? We seem to treat criminals as heroes and police officers as the enemy. Some would go so far as to claim that the current administration has unleashed an unspoken war on the police. Reports of officers cutting back routine police work are rampant. Murder rates in the cities are skyrocketing. Even the home town of our president, Chicago, has seen murders skyrocket since the administration has started their "war" against law enforcement. Trump has expressed support for law enforcement.

There seems to be an almost unlimited number of ways politicians have devised to divide us. Rich-poor, black-white, straight-gay, advantaged-disadvantaged, male-female, Republican-Democrat and on and on. Many Americans are tired of politicians and media elites that seek to divide us for their own purposes. For professional politicians there is much to be gained by division - votes and contributions.

Probably the biggest disappointment of the Obama

reign is the deterioration of race relations. There was a lot of hope that Obama would bring us together rather than seek to tear us apart. He chooses to spend more time with Hollywood celebrities than he does in the inner cities. There is anger on the streets as can be seen virtually every night on the news. Of course people are marching, they see failing schools, no jobs, crime in their neighborhoods and feel alienated from the police. Hell yea they are mad, can you blame them. You see it, I see it and certainly Trump sees it. As Americans we see scenes of marches on the streets way too often. Yes, we are mad about it. Whether marching or watching you would have to be one sick puppy to smile about what is happening. Trump doesn't talk much about differences. He seems to view people as Americans. Rather than seek to divide us he speaks of us as Americans. He doesn't dwell on our differences.

We see the politicians encouraging illegal immigration that further divides us. An effort is being made by politicians to discourage assimilation by new immigrants. The costs of this policy increases our debt and makes it harder for us to find jobs. Trump does not support illegal immigration. Trump doesn't need to stoke division among us to get donations because he is paying for his own campaign. It is refreshing to see a candidate that doesn't seek to categorize and divide us.

People see their country being run by and for the establishment elites and special interests. They are angry about this. Internally generated anger by millions of Americans is nothing new. During the Vietnam War we were angry and took to the streets.

We were protesting the establishment's war. In those days we referred to the establishment as "the man". Well, people got mad enough and "the man" ended the war. Trump is counting on enough people being angry to make big changes in professional politics and our country. Trump seems to be channeling peoples' anger into voter action. His rallies are being attended by throngs of people. The anger is real. Trump's hope is that people will vote for him as an alternative to the corrupt divide and conquer professional politicians.

The Media Elites

"Get your facts first, then you can
distort them as you please."

Mark Twain

Make no mistake the media elites are not your best
friends. They make millions of dollars, they get their
hair and make-up fussed over every day by the
"little" people, they get chauffeured to and fro, they
live in secluded enclaves, they socialize with the 1%
and their children attend private schools. You don't
sit next to them at soccer games, you don't tailgate
with them at football games, you don't wait with
them in a crowded doctor's waiting room and you
certainly don't bump into them at Walmart or
Safeway. Does that make them bad people? Of
course not. It is just that they don't live like you. As
Bill Clinton might say - they don't feel your pain.
How could they? Everything was coming up roses
for these elites until Trump crashed their party.

Main stream media has historically been the domain
of TV, radio and large circulation print such as
magazines and newspapers. Although their
influence has diminished due to the internet it is
nonetheless very influential. It is often referred to as
"the media".   Historically the media attempted to
present an independent view of events that were
unfolding around us. It has morphed into more of an
advocacy tool to present the particular opinion of

those who control the particular media source. The media has been under an assault upon their dominance influence over the publics' view of world events. The internet and alternative media sources have increasingly been attracting peoples' time and attention for years.

The injection of opinion into "news" has turned off many people. The talking heads constantly shouting and interrupting each other has become annoying. They constantly try to tear large groups of us down and divide us. They look unhappy and they sound unhappy. Sometimes while watching them I think I've dozed off and mistakenly turned on the Jerry Springer show. Americans don't like unhappy. Americans like laughter. These media trends have resulted in two significant challenges for the media. Profitability for the media owners has been declining and their influence over the American people is in a state of decline. In plain English they are losing power and money, the opiate of the elites.

No matter if he wins the election or goes down in flames, Trump has changed main stream media as we know it. Is it any wonder that the biggest applause moments at his rallies occur after he attacks the media? Trump pulled back the curtain on the media like Dorothy's dog Toto did to the Wizard of Oz. When Toto pulled back the curtain it revealed an old gasbag speaking into a microphone, not the infallible Wizard that everyone assumed was there. Trump has 8,000,000 followers on twitter. By harnessing the power of social media he is not going to let the media misrepresent him without fighting back.

No single moment illustrates the Trump effect on the media more than the first Fox News Republican debate. The Fox Queen, Megyn Kelly, launched into a vicious attack on Trump in her first tirade posed as a question about his attitude toward women. I suspect that she thought he would cower in her presence and defer to her brilliance. He did not. Trump fought back and exposed her bias against a non-establishment candidate. The game was on! This struck a chord with many people watching the debate. This was what they were waiting for, a person who would not be bullied into looking like the person someone in media tried to paint them as being. Viewers had seen that movie way too many times.

In 2012 CNN's Candy Crowley, posing as a non-biased moderator injected herself into the presidential debate by blatantly taking Obama's side over Romney's. It was particularly evident during a discussion on Benghazi when she defended Obama's truthfulness. Romney did not aggressively stand up for himself. He allowed himself to be bullied. He looked weak. He lost the election. Is there any wonder why people cheered Trump as he took on the Fox team as they tried to weaken his candidacy? The American people don't want a pansy as the leader of the free world. If you can be bullied by "talking heads" how could you possibly defeat ISIS?

Keep in mind that political candidates spend billions of dollars on advertising. The media rely on these ads for profits. Trump is not spending large amounts of money on ads. It would be normal for the media to dislike the lack of ad spending. Trump is getting visibility without the ad spending. He is attracting five, ten, twenty and thirty thousand people to his rallies. He is being shown on TV because people want to hear what he has to say therefore they will watch a program just because he is covered. He is attacking the media because of the way they have acted. It would be normal for the media to be frightened by this type of candidate.

It is quite possible that Fox has permanently damaged their brand by supporting the establishment against Trump. I know that I find it difficult to even turn Fox on after they supported the elites over the people during the primaries. They have simply become the establishment network. CNN has been beating Fox in the prime time ratings for the first time in a decade. It all began with the three Fox debate moderators attacking Trump. They thought they were The Three Musketeers defending the King (Bush) against evil Cardinal Richelieu (Trump). They ended up looking more like The Three Stooges. Fox resisted the new reality to the very end of the primaries. With some exceptions, they supported any establishment candidate in an effort to defeat Trump. They continued to state all the reasons Trump can't win. To this day the numerous Trump haters at Fox continue to frame every question with a not so subtle dig at Trump. Trump and Kelly have stepped up and called a truce to their spat, but the election has a long way to go.

Trump has been on TV almost day and night. Interestingly he has been on CNN and MSNBC on a regular basis. Why is that? CNN and MSNBC have been staunch supporters of democrat candidates for years. It is hard to say. There could be many reasons but none more obvious than an increased number of viewers. My guess is that they witnessed the blunder by the Fox Three Stooges attacking Trump and pounced on it. Or it could be something as devious as thinking he could be easier to beat than a republican establishment candidate. Who cares? The point is that Trump is changing media dynamics by the force of his personality. It seems everyone wants to interview "The Donald". That certainly seems like a good thing. Give the people what they want instead of what you want to give them. Let the voters decide where to go from there. Adapt or die is a fundamental law of nature

I can't watch or read everything the media produces. From my limited perspective the biggest change I've noticed since Trump entered the race has been at CNN. Even the President of CNN has recently said that they may have become too liberal. In my opinion CNN is by far and away the best at coverage of breaking world events and election results. I can't say the same for their regular daily programming. They have been unashamedly biased against traditional American values. At times it almost seems as if CNN is two different networks. One network would be the before and after work programing. The other would be the mid-day (8am-5pm) programming when a different group finally crawl out from under the covers. The before and after work CNN is more respectful of the people who work hard every day. But when the morning rush hour is over, the programming changes dramatically. This time period seems to be the hateful anti-American free-for-all programing block. I have noticed no change in the mid-day programming.

I have noticed a change in the pre and post 8-5 programming. It seems to have changed from the time before Trump and Sanders started to resonate with the American people. I believe they picked up on the anger of working Americans and adapted by addressing people and issues in a more balanced way. No example has been more striking to me than the town hall gun control forum with Obama, that was aired by CNN, and moderated by Anderson Cooper. It was a balanced and civil discussion, even with a highly opinionated President. Honestly, I never thought I would see the day when CNN would present both sides to an issue. Particularly with a President they strongly supported being so vocally on one side of the issue. Has CNN moderated their programming because of the Trump effect on the media? We'll never know.

Trump has also had another important impact on the media. He has called them out for their collusion in the corruption of the election process. No single event illustrates this point more than the removal of the Union Leader newspaper from the republican debate in New Hampshire. The Union Leader is the largest newspaper in New Hampshire. They published a front page editorial insulting Trump. Trump then insisted that they be removed from the "neutral" debate. They were in fact removed by ABC. This may have been an unprecedented display of courage and strength of character by a candidate. Instead of begging for forgiveness he stood his ground and said what needed to have been said for years to the media. Simply, that a clearly biased organization had no business being involved in the electoral debate process. The debate forum is designed to provide the voting public with an opportunity to make decisions regarding the candidates. It is not intended to provide a venue for the media to express their biased opinions.

Not all of the media run in the same herd. Some individuals have built their own brand to a point that they can say, without fear, what they feel is the truth. And quite frankly some see things as they really are more clearly than others. Some examples include Sean Hannity, Bill O'Reilly, Ann Coulter, Lou Dobbs, Mike Gallagher, Joe Scarborough, Laura Ingraham, Stuart Varney and Chris Cuomo. They say what they think without fear of recrimination because they are their own brand. Not unlike Trump, no one is the boss of them. Limbaugh has, as Trump would say, a "huge" audience. But he has damaged his brand by sticking with the elites' line of "the rules are the rules" as Cruz stole delegates from Trump. He failed to realize that the corrupt rules were exactly what people disliked. ABC, NBC, and CBS used to control the "news" airwaves but have now become almost irrelevant. The American public has simply changed the channel after too many years of their biased "news" reporting. Will they adapt? We will see.

Before we can understand the Trump Movement we have to wipe our slate clean of what we are told to believe by the media. They are powerful enablers of the current political system. They benefit from leaving things the way they are. By the time you read this book much may have changed. Trump may be on the way to victory in the election. If that is the case the media establishment elites will be jumping on the Trump train with both feet. If they don't, they risk losing their influence, power and money.

For as long as I can remember the media has put a liberal slant on questions they ask non-liberal politicians. Media Trump haters start their "questions" with a negative innuendo about Trump. Historically, non-liberal politicians have quietly let the media put a less than truthful spin on issues during interviews for fear of being smeared. That is all changing because of Donald Trump. Two examples I witnessed just today illustrate the point. I witnessed the Governor of North Carolina being interviewed on CNBC about the transgender bathroom issue. CNBC started the interview by saying "hundreds of businesses are boycotting North Carolina". The Governor forcefully made the point that the CNBC statement was blatantly false. A republican Senator has asked Facebook to explain why they delete "conservative" stories from their trending news feed. By others stepping forward as these politicians have done will only multiply the Trump effect.

What makes Them So Special?

> "When I have to choose between voting for the people or the special interests, I always stick with the special interests. They remember. The people forget."

Henry F. Ashurst

Does your government make you feel special? Didn't think so. Donald Trump feels he does not need to take money from anyone to be elected President. Therefore, he doesn't owe anything to anyone except the people of this country for the privilege of serving as their president. That is a really easy concept for voters to understand. It is also a very appealing concept to voters. The slang in America is rife with implicit and explicit references to this concept. Just a few are: don't bite the hand that feeds you, got your six, you scratch my back and I'll scratch yours and quid pro quo. All meaning you do something for me and I expect to do something for you. My favorite is the Detroit City Councilwoman who shouted "bring home the bacon" as she explained how Obama owed them because they voted for him. Can you see anything wrong with this concept? Of course not.

Trump can and does say whatever he wants

because he can. He is financially independent and emotionally secure. He does not need their money to get elected. He quite frankly doesn't appear to care what someone thinks about him. This is radically different than recent candidates for president. They pander for votes changing what they say from speech to speech, depending on the audience, because they need their votes. They vote for positions backed by their special interest donors because they need their money. Trump is ushering in a seminal change in political campaigning and it has the establishment terrified.

"Special Interests" are nothing more than people or organizations that have their own interests as their primary concern. It is arguably legal, certainly expected and almost encouraged by our current political system to bestow favors for votes and contributions. There doesn't seem to be anything wrong with that as long as you are not causing any harm. Ah but there's the rub. Our political system has become so corrupted that a special interest's gain almost always becomes someone else's loss. We seem to have lost the balance that our elected officials have been hired to maintain. That is heart of the corruption problem. Some politicians lose sight of the harm caused by the favors they bestow upon special interests. They do not strike a balance between the negative impacts on the people they were elected to represent with the positive impact to the special interest.

A minnow named the Delta smelt versus the people of California is just such a case in point regarding the balancing of special interests. Nobody really knows how many Delta smelt actually exist in the

San Joaquin River delta, but the number is estimated to be a few hundred to a few dozens. These minnows are probably the most expensive creatures ever to grace our planet. Politicians, at the insistence of their "environmentalists" friends and supporters, have made it so. In a failing effort to save this minnow the Feds have mandated that rainwater flow straight through rivers, unused, into the ocean.

Let's not cry over a little spilt water for the minnows you say. How does a couple trillion gallons grab you? Yup, you can put your reading glasses back, you read that right, trillion with a T. That's potentially how many gallons the feds have insisted be sent into the ocean to try and save a few minnows. Meanwhile California is in a dire water shortage. An area of rich farmland the size of Rhode Island is now a dustbowl and can no longer be farmed for a lack of water. Just think about how many people that would feed. Or, the water could be used to sustain more than 5 million people. Instead the special interests insist that we throw farmers out of work, increase the cost of food crops and implement a water state of emergency in California. All costing us tens of billions of dollars on top of the lifestyle restrictions placed on the people of California. If these radical environmentalists were in power throughout the world, we would all starve to death. Trump has addressed this particular issue during a speech in California. He basically said this madness has got to stop and will stop if he is elected.

Although it may seem each special interest group is favored by one party or the other, that is not necessarily true. Wall Street is a perfect example.

Most people probably believe the republicans are the preferred party of Wall Street. That is not true. Recently they have given more donations to the democrats. Hillary talks about fighting for you against wall street after having raked in millions of dollars for giving "top secret speeches" to wall street firms. How's that going to work? Yea, I'm heading to Vegas to place a bet that wall street will beat out the little guy, even though Hillary will have fought so valiantly for them. It's all about gaining influence wherever it resides. For many, but not all special interest groups, it means supporting both parties. Suffice it to say, politicians are all feeding at the special interest donation trough.

The pharmaceutical industry is a particularly glaring rich and powerful example of a special interest group. No one would argue that the development of new, safer and more effective medicines is not a worthwhile cause. But many Americans would argue that it is not fair that Americans pay 2 times, 4 times, 10 times or more for the same prescriptions than everyone else in the world. Why is that? Because our politicians insist that we pay more to the pharmaceutical companies. We actually have laws that prohibit our government from negotiating lower drug prices for drugs paid for by the taxpayers. Other countries have laws prohibiting the drug companies from charging over a certain amount. In short, we pay higher prices and the rest of the world pays lower prices. Trump has said he would negotiate lower prices for us.

Even more egregious, U.S. based pharmaceutical companies are moving their headquarters and jobs overseas in order to pay less in taxes to the U.S.

These moves contribute to a sky rocketing national deficit, lost jobs and millions of elderly Americans plunged into poverty as a result of mandated high prescription drug costs. Recently they have also exerted their influence to allow 11-year-old children to receive opiate based prescriptions, the gateway to heroin addiction. Reflect on that for a moment. Your elected representatives are working hand-in-hand with drug companies to increase the use of opiates among younger and younger children. The result will be increased profits and campaign contributions along with a spike in childhood addition.

No matter where you stand on Obamacare some things are crystal clear. Medical costs for Americans are soaring. Insurance premiums and deductibles are increasing dramatically. Insurance company profits are at record highs. Special interest groups at work once again. Most of the thousands of Obamacare regulations were designed and drafted by the special interest lobbyists. Corrupt politics at its finest! Special interests get what they want and politicians get what they want. Win-win. But what about the people who pay the bills? Guess we should have hired a lobbyist.

Let's talk briefly about education. The teachers' and administrators' union bosses are very influential people in our electoral process. They control vast sums of union dues from their members. They also have influence over their members' opinions. They are the Goliath of the special interests in the gigantic education system. Through donations and thought influence (votes) for their preferred politicians they have helped shape our existing educational system. As a result, our nation spends significantly more to educate a student than any nation in the world. Yet our student performance lags sorely behind many other countries. I find it hard to believe that our teachers are not as talented as any in the world. They just need to be allowed to do their job.

Burdensome governmental regulations are a primary reason education costs have been driven up to unconscionable levels. Politicians have learned that the best way to influence people is to control what they are taught. They do this by regulating what is acceptable and what is not. This practice is nothing new, totalitarian regimes have used this tactic throughout history. Universities support the politicians that benefit them. A case in point is a $300,000 speaking fee paid by UCLA to Hillary, now a current presidential candidate. How's that for buying influence? That money could have been better used to reduce the cost of education for all students.

Many special interests have a hand in this problem. They range from student loan lenders to university administrators. There is virtually no one speaking out for the families and students that have to pay or borrow for a college education. Many students are saddled with student loans that they may never be able to pay off. Many are precluded from buying a house due to the student loans hanging over their heads. I recently paid $450 just for a parking pass for my son to attend a university. That is almost as much as I paid for a full year of tuition when I was in school! This is what happens when virtually all the special interests are lined up on the side of spending. Students and families lack a strong advocate for their needs that include reducing the costs.

These are but a few examples of special interest groups at work. There are literally thousands more but you get the idea. There are as many on the "left" as there are on the "right". The financial cartel, covered in another chapter, is by far the largest and most powerful. None of these groups necessarily have bad intentions. They are simply playing the hand that was dealt to them. They could just as easily work more for the benefit of the American people if that was the way the game (system) was designed. Even within our system they manage to make great contributions to mankind.

Let's be clear, Trump has legally donated large sums of money to obtain political influence. Trump is a very successful international businessman. He couldn't thrive in our system of free enterprise if he didn't play the game the way it is designed. It would be similar to fighting with one arm tied behind your back. Trump has donated money to politicians of both parties. He has even donated money to the Clintons. Get over it. It does not mean that he agrees with all their political views.

Donald Trump, if elected President, would start from a position of not owing any special interest favors to anyone for their contributions. He is also a master negotiator. He even wrote a bestselling book "The Art of the Deal". His business accomplishments speak to his ability to bring parties with different interests together and reach a mutually favorable outcome. No one could build skyscrapers though out the world if they could not. Professional politicians simply cannot do this because of their need to favor special interests in order to be elected. No wonder many people feel that Trump is the answer to ending the special interests' painful domination of their daily lives.

The Wall Street/Washington Cartel

"I believe that banking institutions
are more dangerous to our liberties
than standing armies."

Thomas Jefferson

The Wall Street-Washington cartel is the mother of all special interest groups. It is also unique in that the professional politicians can double dip into the money pot. First, they receive large donations from Wall Street while in office or while seeking office. Then they can work for, or get paid for giving speeches to Wall Street firms when they leave office. Nice gig if you can get it. If I were to write a screenplay about the Wall Street-Washington cartel it would be a gangster movie. Unfortunately, it would contain no drama since all their activities are carried out in the open for everyone to see.

Their lavish lifestyles are open for everyone to see. Nowhere is this more apparent than when hordes of private jets descend on luxurious destinations such as Davos, Switzerland and Jackson Hole, Wyoming. Our public servants, accompanied by their Wall Street friends attend conferences to plot their next moves to increase the power of the cartel. All in the name of helping to create a better economy for everyone. The results speak for themselves.

Attendees will spend more in a few days than a family would pay to have a wedding for a son or daughter. Is it any wonder why our public servants fight so hard to become part of this elite group?

This chapter is in no way intended to imply all politicians and government employees are involved in or agree with the cartel's nefarious activities. I have to believe the vast majority of government employees work hard to do the right thing for the right reason. Senator Paul is an example of a politician fighting hard against the cartel for the American public. Unfortunately, the cartel holds the balance of power. In fact, they are so large and powerful that I needed to sub-title this chapter.

How it Works

In brief here is how it works. The Wall Street banks, hedge funds and private equity firms make enormous contributions to politicians to the tune of billions of dollars. Wall Street can also give high paying jobs to ex-office holders and ex-employees of governmental regulating agencies. On top of that, the lucky few at the pinnacle of the food chain can receive very generous speaking fees to the tune of hundreds of thousands of dollars per speech from Wall Street firms after they leave government employment. Hillary raked in $21,000,000 from speaking engagements, mostly from wall street, in just two years. One has to include the Federal Reserve as a member in good standing of this cartel. No one really knows what the heck this organization truly is. Suffice it to say that they have thousands of employees with salaries totaling over a billion dollars and exert enormous influence over our citizens. These employees enjoy average salaries of over $70,000 per year, greatly exceeding the average salaries of the citizens they "serve".

So what does the Wall Street gang receive for their money? Enormous wealth and freedom from prosecution for criminal acts to start with. I don't have to go into a lot of detail on the income inequality in this country driven by the cartel. You see it and you feel it. A recent study showed that the wealthiest 62 people in the world had as much wealth as the poorest 3.6 billion people in the world. Read it again, it is not a typo. In case you think it doesn't matter, consider the following. Income inequality is the currently the worst it has been since the late 1920's which marked the start of the Great Depression. Kind of depressing isn't it! The Wall Street gang reels in huge amounts of booty as a result of our government's role in their activities. And you very, very rarely see one of them spend a day in jail as a result of their countless activities that break laws. Unbelievably a recent Attorney General of the United States as much as said that they are simply too big to prosecute for crimes.

A Huge Scheme - The Housing Bubble

The Housing Bubble created by the cartel is a perfect illustration. The cartel fueled a huge boom in housing during the last decade. Incalculable amounts of money were made by the Wall Street gang. The politicians were happy because jobs were being created and they were getting reelected. People were happy as their homes went up in value. They were encouraged to borrow freely against their homes from the banks and spend, spend, spend.

They created "liar loans" and "NINJA"(no income no job no assets) loans. All the while our regulators turned a blind eye to newspaper headlines describing the situation. Fortunes were made and laws were broken. It was all a charade, organized by the cartel, that came crashing down on the heads of the American public. You know what happened next, millions of people lost their homes, bankers were thrown in jail, politicians were thrown out of office and regulators were fired. Err not exactly. Yes, millions of Americans did have their homes foreclosed and suffered greatly. The rest of the story worked out quite differently.

Wall Street executives continued to enjoy generous salaries and bonuses while their employees were being laid off left and right. Professional politicians continued to get reelected, after all who could have seen the bust coming? Regulators continued to receive their generous salaries at the expense of the very citizens that suffered from the bust. Ex-politicians and ex-regulators continued to get their cushy jobs and lavish speaking fees from Wall Street. The next member of the Wall Street gang that goes to jail for their part in illegal activities related to the housing scheme will be the first I have heard of. Similarly, the next regulator that gets fired for their actions or lack of action will also be the first I've heard of.

The Wall Street Poster Child

For some reason the investment firm of Goldman Sachs seems to have become the poster child of the intertwined relationship between Wall Street and Washington. Here is just a tiny sample of some of the relationships:

- Goldman paid Hillary $675,000 for just 3 speeches,

- Ted Cruz's wife is on leave from employment at Goldman,

-Several former Goldman chairmen have served as Treasury Secretary of the United States,

-Goldman has employed a multitude of former Securities and Exchange Commission public servants (the SEC is the "watchdog" of the securities industry),

-Former Goldman executives directed the efforts of the $700 billion Wall Street bailout,

-Goldman employees reputedly contributed more money to electing Obama than any other company,

-Goldman has dozens of ex-governmental employees on staff working as lobbyists,

-Former Federal Reserve officials have been employed or received speaking fees from Goldman,

This list is just the tip of the iceberg but you get the idea. And Goldman is far from alone among Wall Street firms. The fox is guarding the Treasury hen-house. I can't emphasize enough how small a sample this list is. Just these few examples should be enough to cause anyone to wonder what the heck is going on here. Not to say Goldman is any better or worse that dozens of other firms but they may be the most visible. I can't judge the motives of the tens of thousands of people involved in these relationships over the years. I'm sure many positive things have resulted from the cross pollination of Washington and Wall Street.

Crime and Punishment

What happens if the intertwined relationships are not so positive? The punishment for the gang members for their nefarious actions are merely fines. Hardly a person loses a job. The fines levied on the Wall Street gang have added up to over $40 billion dollars. The aforementioned Goldman Sacks has recently, reputedly, to have agreed to a $5 billion fine for their part in the housing bubble mortgage fraud scheme. Ok, so the bad guys got punished. Not so fast. First of all, the fines were paid primarily by their companies. Secondly, the profits they hauled in from their activities usually exceeded the fines. If fact billions in fines continue to be levied on the gang for various new and different nefarious activities since the housing bubble scheme. Once again they break the law and get fined for an amount less then they raked in. I think that fact that fines for new activities continue to happen tells us that they make a net profit on the activities after paying the fine.

Try stealing from a convenience store and see if you are simply asked to pay a fine in an amount less than what you stole, instead of spending time in jail. What would stop someone from stealing more everyday if they only had to pay a fine for a lessor amount. Nice work if you can get it. That is how the game is played. That is the result of a completely corrupt government participating within a corrupt cartel. Now if you really want to get angry, consider that these fines are tax deductible. That's right, the fines are reduced by savings in taxes paid. As a bonus the professional politicians also get to claim they are doing their job by collecting these fines.

The Federal Reserve

The Federal Reserve's role in ongoing cartel activities is a bit harder to understand. Yes, they get their jobs and speaking fees from the investment gangs. They may turn a blind eye to nefarious activities. But the damage they do is systematic. The Federal Reserve is supposed to help keep inflation under control and help to create jobs - the "dual mandate". To give you an idea of how good a job they doing with inflation consider the following. If someone had one U.S. dollar at the inception of the Federal Reserve, it could now buy something worth one penny in today's economy. In other words, inflation has eaten away 99% of your buying power. Not so good. Bad news for you but good news for the cartel. It would take too long to explain why but I think the fact that Wall Street firms are raking in record profits is proof enough.

Want more proof? As the Fed has driven interest rates down, savers and the elderly are being punished by being paid virtually nothing in interest on their life's savings while the gang prospers? The Federal Reserve is pushing savers into risky Wall Street schemes that inevitably collapse and leave them holding the bag. If the gang just needs to park some of the loot they get from savers' zero interest bank accounts and money market deposits, the Fed will gladly pay the gang interest on your money. There is even talk of "negative interest rates" where you will have to pay the banks for the privilege of them hanging onto your money. It's happening in Europe and Japan right now. Just doesn't smell right does it?

The recent oil boom engineered by the cartel is a current example. Oil prices have been driven to record high prices, made possible by the availability of free money. Huge amounts of savers money are then pushed into the hands of the cartel for risky energy investment schemes. Then the price of oil collapses causing huge losses to the unwary investors. They have also been hard at work on an automobile bubble. Drive sales of autos to record numbers by the availability of easy, cheap loans. Expand the terms of the loans to 8 years making payments lower. Finance the auto, the sales taxes and fees, generous trade in allowances plus a cash bonus for buying the car. The end result is a consumer driving out the door with a 5 to 8-year loan in an amount 20%-40% more than what they could sell the car for. Just like the housing bubble the financial companies make a fortune and the consumers will be crying in their Toyota in a few years. Rinse and repeat. Who knows what will be next.

We haven't even discussed derivatives. Derivatives is a fancy word for made up financial assets of almost unlimited varieties like swaps, forwards, options and so on. The nominal amount of derivatives could exceed some quadrillion dollars. A quadrillion is 1,000 trillion. No one knows how much for certain since it is a complex, and for the most part unregulated market. This has only been made possible by Central Banks around the world creating the liquidity conditions that enable unlimited derivatives to be created. A well-known billionaire investor has likened them to a time bomb and weapons of mass destruction. While a former Federal Reserve Chairman has stated that the derivatives market has become so large because it provides economic value to their users. The users in this case would be the cartel. If this baby blows up, it is game over! It won't matter who you vote for. Trump has said that he would demand to know just what the Federal Reserve is up to.

The Great Job Killing Machine

The cartel has become a great job killing machine. Regulations driven by special interests of all flavors are strangling economic enterprise in this country. The regulations make it difficult for businesses to create or keep jobs in this country. The regulations have helped to drive growth to a standstill in this country, with growth being picked up by less regulated countries like China. The regulatory war on Americans has driven up the cost of everything made in America that we consume or use. Meanwhile wages are decreasing as businesses can no longer compete if they have to pay a living wage to American workers.

In light of decreasing or declining domestic growth the cartel has adjusted. The cartel needs higher stock and investment prices to thrive. The Federal Reserve plays a critical role in this scheme. The centerpiece of the solution is to print tons of money and price it at zero. The Federal Reserve has done just that. The gang members and corporations can borrow money at virtually zero interest rates. By the way, that means you receive a zero interest return on your savings. This free money is the gas that powers the scheme. Sadly, this gas was previously used in measured amounts to drive job creation.

Jobs as a percentage of the population are declining. They can make up any statistics they want such as the very manipulated unemployment rate. That doesn't change the fact that fewer working age Americans are working full-time than at any time in decades. And many of those who want to work are only able to get part-time jobs. A mass of regulations has helped to fuel part-time employment. The mother of which is Obamacare. Whatever else Obamacare has accomplished, it has thrown many people into part-time employment and sent insurance company stocks to record highs.

Using only stock prices as an example, I will roughly outline how the free money scheme works to kill jobs. Even as the free money fuel has recently driven stock prices to record highs it applies to other types of investments as well. Wall Street packages "free" money in the form of debt that corporations issue. Much of this debt issued by corporations is called "covenant lite", meaning the borrowing conditions are less strict thereby reducing the chances that it can be paid back. This covenant lite debt sets the stage for yet another bailout by the public. The money received from the debt is then used to buy back the corporation's own stock. The amount of stock outstanding is reduced therefore the price of the stock goes up. Additionally, regulators allow companies to deceive the public about how much money they actually earn. Companies are freely allowed to tout to investors their "adjusted earnings". Adjusted earnings are shorthand for excluding many costs of doing business. Therefore, earnings look higher than they actually are from a historical perspective. Once again stock prices go up, without the need for companies to create jobs and grow.

Companies are also shifting jobs to other countries to take advantage of lower labor costs. Labor costs are lower in other countries for many reasons. People will work for less because their cost of living is less. A significant and direct reason relates to the regulations that are killing jobs in this country. In many countries companies can employ people without regard to workers' health care, safety of their working environment and their age and hours worked per day. Also, companies don't need to worry about the environmental impact of their factories. The list of regulations they escape is as endless as the millions of pages of regulations in this country. Companies earn more profits and stock prices go up by shifting jobs elsewhere. The ugly truth is that the regulations we care so deeply about can be avoided by moving American jobs to other countries.

The latest innovation out of Wall Street is an activity called "Inversions". Many countries have lower income tax rates than we do. Many American companies are now shifting their legal headquarters to other countries. They do this by buying or merging with the foreign company. They then move numbers of corporate employees to the foreign country. This inversion results in the company paying less in taxes. Earnings go up and likewise stock prices go up. Jobs in America go down along with our tax receipts from corporations. Trump has said he will stop inversions in two seconds.

Politicians Have Their Back.

The damage done to our financial system by the cartel is enormous. By creating yet another stock market bubble we are setting the stage for another bailout. Our professional politicians regularly bail out the banks and corporations like General Motors after every scheme blows up. These bailouts amount to hundreds of billions of dollars. There is no incentive for the gang to change if there are no consequences for failure. Our politicians are the enablers of these schemes. The professional politicians refuse to reel in the activities of the secretive Federal Reserve. They allow the Federal Reserve to manipulate interest rates and create enormous amounts of money for two primary reasons. First, it allows the Wall Street gang to create massive wealth for themselves. Secondly, it allows the government to borrow money cheaply.

The politicians can also spend more if it costs less in interest to borrow the money on the debt they ring up. If we paid just 1% more on our $19 trillion in debt that would be $190 billion more of interest, we would pay. And that additional interest would have to be added to new debt every year. If we paid 2% more, that would amount to $380 billion every year. Now you get the idea why the professional politicians want us to earn nothing on our savings.

Everybody's Talking About the Good Old Days

It didn't always used to be this way. Banks have been an integral contributor to our economic strength. They made sound loans that helped borrowers prosper and create jobs. I think it is fair to say that we wouldn't be an economic powerhouse without them. This was accomplished primarily through local and regional banks. They were smaller, close to the people and did not exert control over federal government officials. They expected to be repaid for the loans they made. The old style local and regional banks are now in the process of being driven out of business as a result of the burdens of the back-breaking government regulations. Their activities are being consolidated in the hands of the Wall Street gang that can afford to pay for the costs of regulations. As smaller banks disappear, the circle of corruption is being expanded.

Can and will even "The Donald" change it

The simple answer is that he alone cannot disarm the cartel of mass destruction if he is elected president. He can begin to sanitize it. But he and he alone among active candidates has unique attributes that would allow him to make a difference. He knows the cartel game inside and out. He has bought influence from politicians of all flavors. Nothing quite sums it up as his answer as to why Mrs. Clinton was at his wedding. "She really had no choice because I gave to a (her) foundation." Trump has operated within the highest levels of the elites. He can speak their language. He does not need lucrative speaking fees or donations to a family foundation. He is already rich. He does not need to resist the temptations of the cartel; he is not even tempted to begin with.

Trump appears to be the only candidate to recognize, or to tell the truth, that we are in a bubble. A new bubble created by the cartel, and for the cartel. The current brewing financial bubble has been enabled by the central banks of the world. They have allowed the world financial system to float on the "carry trade". It is making fortunes for the elites while not helping the middle class. The carry trade is simply borrowing money at a low rate of return and "investing" at a higher rate of return. The central banks are manipulating interest and currency rates around the world. This allows the cartel to borrow money cheaper in one country (Japan) and "invest" it at a higher rate of return in another country (U.S.). The central banks do whatever is necessary to make it a risk free scheme for the cartel. It is really nothing more than an electronic money shell game.

Fortunes are being made by the elites. There are always losers in a rigged game, that would be us. The bubble is in all the high priced assets controlled by the elites. Consider over-the-top mansions. There are as many as 50 mansions available for sale in the world for over $100 million dollars. You're going to love this example offered by fashion magnate, Pierre Cardin. His French Riviera property, "Le Palais Bulles" is listed at around $450 million. The English translation for the name is, wait for it, "The **Bubble** Palace"! So the bubble is helping the elites but not ordinary people. But you can bet when it blows up that the little guy will be stuck with the bill.

If you don't think a rich republican would really look out for the average guy, consider republican President Teddy Roosevelt. He was born into a wealthy family but went on to become the original progressive President. He championed a "Square Deal" policy for the average American. It can be done and it has been done. Wall Street, our government employees and our corporate leaders stand ready to build a job creating machine if only our system would encourage them to do so. Trump would unleash our best and brightest to do just that.

No Wall for You

"It is not in the stars to hold our
destiny but in ourselves"

William Shakespeare

It's not that the elites don't see the value and need for walls. They just feel that walls for you are not in their best interests. Several examples illustrate the hypocrisy of the elite's spoken attitude about the appropriateness of a wall on our southern border.

Even the Pope has weighed in on Trump's proposal to build a wall. No surprise, he is against it, calling it "not Christian". The Pope lives within Vatican City, a 110-acre sovereign state. Most of Vatican City is surrounded by massive walls and it is all heavily guarded. Can you even image the Vatican if homeless people, terrorists and criminals had free access to the Vatican? It wouldn't survive one week of open borders.

Mark Zuckerberg, CEO of Facebook, has also weighed in on the wall issue. He warned about "fearful voices" calling for a wall. Not only does Zuckerberg have his home walled off from the masses but he also bought the 4 houses surrounding his home for additional privacy. He has also bought a 700-acre property in Kauai for extreme privacy when he hits the beach. Seems like he isn't fond of mixing with the hordes of illegals crossing our borders.

The ultimate irony is the Secret Service calling for higher fences to protect the White House. The hypocrisy is deafening. So there you have it. The walls are good for us (the elites) but not for you.

How about other nations? Trump is being criticized by the international community for proposing a wall. The ancestral home of Obama, Kenya, is building a wall along the Somalia border to control the flow of radical Islamic terrorists. Tunisia, with support from U.S. taxpayers, is building a border wall between it and Libya to control the illegal migration of terrorists. We probably should help them with this, as it was Hillary's nation building in Libya that created the terrorist problem in Libya. You can only laugh at this next one. Mexico has built a wall on their southern border with Guatemala to restrict the flow of illegal immigrants into Mexico! In fact, the entire world is plastered with walls and fences.

There has been a lot of laughter at Trump's assertion that Mexico will pay for the wall. Trump is a professional developer and has estimated the cost at $10 billion. Trump says Mexico reaps a trade surplus of $58 billion with us every year, partially because the Mexican leaders are smarter than Obama. On top of that, untold billions are sent back to Mexico from Mexicans in our country. The billions sent back are earned from the drug trade, under the table wages (untaxed) and our generous social benefit paid to illegals. Quite frankly, the Mexican economy would collapse without our trade. A president Trump would have incredible power over

Mexico. He could virtually throw their country into chaos if they refused to pay. They would pay the $10 billion in a heartbeat. As an aside, Mexico paying for the wall draws the biggest applause at his rallies.

Let's just get the physical construction of the wall question out of the way. Trump building a wall on a mostly wasteland southern boarder would be like your child playing with Legos. Anyone who would have you believe that it is impossible or impractical to build a wall is simply not telling the truth or is naively unaware of great American accomplishments. Until a wall is built we will not control the destiny of our country. If you need proof, you simply need to examine wall-less Europe becoming overwhelmed by crime and terror from masses of "refugees".

The following are words spoken by President Franklin D. Roosevelt 80 years ago at the Dedication of the Boulder (later the Hoover) dam.

"We are here to celebrate the completion of the greatest dam in the world, rising 726 feet above the bedrock of the river and altering the geography of a whole region: we are here to see the creation of the largest artificial lake in the world-115 miles long, holding enough water, for example, to cover the whole State of Connecticut to a depth of ten feet; and we are here to see nearing completion a power house which will contain the largest generators and turbines yet installed in this country, machinery that can continuously supply nearly two million horsepower of electric energy."

President Franklin D. Roosevelt continued, "This morning I came, I saw, and I was conquered, as everyone would be who sees for the first time this great feat of mankind. . .. Ten years ago the place where we gathered was an unpeopled, forbidding desert. In the bottom of the gloomy canyon whose precipitous walls rose to heights of more than a thousand feet, flowed a turbulent, dangerous river. . . .. The site of Boulder City was a cactus-covered waste. And the transformation wrought here in these years is a twentieth century marvel." Speech by Roosevelt at the Dedication of Boulder Dam, September 30, 1935.

I have stood on the top of this dam and it is stunning. Words alone cannot explain the absolute scope and scale of this American accomplishment. A feeling of awe overtook me as I stood on top of 3,250,000 cubic yards of concrete almost 100 stories high above the largest water reservoir in the country. This dam was constructed in just 5 years. Keep in mind that this was during the 1930s. We had no computers and none of our modern mammoth construction equipment. By the way it only cost $49 million to complete.

I have also stood at the top of the Empire State Building. It also offers a breath-taking view. This building was completed 85 years ago in 1931. It took less than two years to build at a cost of $41,000,000. It stands 102 stories, has 73 elevators and at the time was the tallest building in the world. Once again there were no computers to aid in the design, planning and construction of this magnificent building. There were not the modern cranes and other equipment to use during the construction. Amazing.

On September 12, 1962, President John F. Kennedy famously said during a speech "We choose to go to the moon". Seven years later on July 20, 1969 Apollo 11 became the first manned mission to land on the moon. How's that for American "can do" attitude in action.

All three of these great American accomplishments created tens of thousands of American jobs. They were examples of our "can do" attitude, imagination and innovation. They were completed many years ago without the technological advantages we currently enjoy. Please don't feel people are so stupid as to believe we can't build a wall.

If we choose not to build a wall on our southern border it is quite simply because we don't want to do it.

The Global Warming Money Grab

I'm saying, Come on, the global warming thing? How did the ice melt during the ice ages? Was the dinosaurs driving SUVs around back then?

Larry the Cable Guy

Alternative energy is all the craze lately. Understandably it is the current gold standard for special interest groups. There is more pork to be had than on all the pig farms in America. And more votes to be obtained than at an open bar, free chicken dinner at a political rally. It is large, technologically complex and confusing. Many people, myself included, care passionately about it. And it may or may not be critical to our future.

For those of you who believe the science is settled on global warming, chill-out. Special interest groups can be deceptive sometimes. During the 1970s we were scared of global cooling. We were actually hard at work designing ways to make the earth warmer. We were designing reflective dishes that we would put into orbit to deflect heat onto the earth. The earth was much warmer during Medieval times. The earth is no warmer today than it has been at times during each of the last two decades.

Global warming proponents have been caught "faking" results in their "scientific" studies. Let's just say the science isn't settled, it's the large flow of money to proponents that is settled. It is large and it is real.

The alternative energy special interest group includes environmentalists, academicians, oil companies, railroads, pipelines, automobile companies and a list too long to detail. Technologies and energy sources involved range from hydrocarbons to solar to wind to electric cars and a multitude of others. The example of Tesla is a perfect case in point. Tesla makes electric cars for people that can afford to pay $100,000+ for a car. The founder of the company is now a billionaire donor of the democrats. The people of America have paid for all this by governmental grants, tax credits and the like. In summary we turned a donor into a billionaire and subsidized expensive cars. We are further in debt while Tesla burns through billions of our cash. And by the way, those cars plug into our carbon energy based electrical system to recharge. Several more paragraphs will only cover the tip of the iceberg (pun intended).

As we discuss alternative energy it is important to remember we have an alternative right under our feet. The U.S. has more natural gas than any country on earth. Natural gas vehicle technology could be implemented quickly and it would create American jobs. It is a really cheap fuel source, many times cleaner than oil and could produce significant American jobs. In fact, a nighttime satellite image of gas-producing areas of our country reflects bright images of natural gas being burned off unused at the wellheads. So why don't we choose to save money, have a cleaner environment right now and create American jobs? Why wouldn't "environmentalists" rather have natural gas, that is being burned unused, utilized instead of dirtier, imported oil as a fuel source. You guessed it, there are more political donations and votes to be had if we don't. The thinking seems to be that if we could solve the perceived problem that easily, a lot of government dollars would not be available to special interest donors with alternative solutions.

Clean coal technology has progressed to the point that as high as 80-90% of carbon emissions can be captured when burning coal. Yet Obama and Hillary are waging a war against domestic coal usage. Hillary even gleefully announced that she would be putting American coal miners out of jobs. Meanwhile, they appear to be fine with buying oil from the Middle East. They also appear to be fine with higher energy bills for us as they switch to higher priced sources of energy.

Let's take the issue of Iowa and ethanol since it plays such a big part in our political process. Winning the Iowa presidential primary is critical to the multitude of politicians who dream of becoming president. Ethanol is a fuel additive that can be made from corn, quite a bit of which is grown in Iowa. It is important to the farming lobbyists. Seems like a worthwhile environmental cause if it makes the environment cleaner and reduces the amount of oil used notwithstanding that it costs us more. Unfortunately, things are not as clear as they may seem. The production and transportation of ethanol uses approximately the same amount of fossil fuels as it saves at the gas pump. So no benefit there. The production of ethanol uses tremendous amounts of scarce water. Ethanol production also does considerable damage to the environment due to the large amounts of fertilizers used to grow the corn. The Mississippi river delta used to be the richest marine life area of our continental coastline. It is now a dead zone. It has been polluted primarily by the fertilizer residue flowing down the Mississippi river from the crop growing states. Not very friendly to the environment. The cost of food for Americans has increased as we use corn for fuel rather than food.

How about solar power and electric cars? They are both highly inefficient sources of energy. Why do we pay tens of thousands of taxpayer dollars for every Tesla electric car bought by taxpayers? Why do we generously subsidize solar panels made in China? These are hugely unprofitable enterprises run by large, primarily democrat, political donors. The founders and owners of these enterprises have made billion dollar personal fortunes driven by the various governmental subsidies. Meanwhile, your taxes, our national debt and costs of using energy have risen. Just saying.

Then there is taxpayer subsidized wind power. Trump has talked about this. Wind power kills thousands, probably millions, of birds. No problem for the government as these wind farms are owned by billionaire democrat donors. Any non-wind company slaughtering birds would have the government suing them left and right.

We would rather transport oil in ships, subject to

spills, from far away countries, some of whom support terrorism, than use our domestic sources. It seems that we oppose cheap domestic sources just to keep the money flowing to special interests; the big oil companies that have interests in foreign oil production and the multitude of alternative energy special interests. Rather than use more pipelines, we transport oil and natural gas by railroads, powered by hydrocarbons, that often experience spills causing damage to our environment. Opposition to the Keystone pipeline is a high profile example. Even the government concedes it would be a better environmental alternative than railroads. Turns out that a billionaire railroad owner is a large contributor and supporter of influential democrat politicians.

As a country we have gone down a path of treating American oil, natural gas and coal as inherently evil sources of energy. This has happened even as technology has made the production, transportation and use of hydrocarbons safer, cheaper and more environmentally clean. We have blindly gone full steam into alternative energy without consideration of the consequences to all aspects of the environment or the tremendous cost to the public. So called "environmentalists" are fighting relentlessly to keep energy jobs out of our country. Meanwhile we are buying solar panels from China and oil from Saudi Arabian oilfields developed by the Binladin family. (does that name sound familiar?) In many cases we seem to be doing the wrong thing for what the public has been led (told) to believe is the right reason.

The Political Correctness Scourge

"The Framers of the Constitution knew that free speech is the friend of change and revolution, but they also knew that it is always the deadliest enemy of tyranny."

Hugo Black

Trump has unquestionably opened a dialog on issues people are concerned about. Over my lifetime, dialog about serious issues has regressed into arguments about what can be discussed and what cannot. The concept of "political correctness" has been thrust upon us by a vocal minority. It has suppressed the free speech of Americans for fear of being called out as an unworthy human being. Now, people shout rather than listen. Trump is unafraid to say what he thinks. He has opened dialog about the issues that people feel need to be discussed. Millions of American people are opening their windows and shouting "let's talk about it". It is hard to believe that most people agree with everything Trump says. They just want things openly discussed and resolved for the better. All of our liberties flow from freedom of speech. If speech is repressed, you can bet our other liberties will also be repressed. Remember that we are only one Supreme Court Justice away from losing these liberties.

I just have to talk about Trump using the "L" word. That would be Liar, or a Trump derivative, lyin'. Merriam-Webster defines lie, the verb; to make an untrue statement with intent to deceive, or to create a false, or misleading impression. Reread that definition, isn't that exactly what politicians and the media have been doing? The media would have you believe that anyone using this word (Trump) is being vulgar. I believe that by calling a rat - a rat, Trump has set us free. If we begin to force the media and politicians to tell the truth, we are truly on the road to ending corruption in this country. Corruption is like a mushroom; it only grows in the dark. The media and politicians have had a gentleman's agreement that the word lie should not be used against each other, thereby keeping the people in the dark. Therefore, they all get away with lying. I say bring it on! Let's call out the liars for their actions and force them to tell the truth.

The Federal Government is now pushing "Common Core" on our schools. Make no mistake, this is an effort to teach our children what to believe and what to think. It may be a baby step but it is morphing into the control of our schools by a small group of politicians who will inevitably force their personal ideas and beliefs onto our children. It has happened in totalitarian societies throughout history and it will happen here if left unchecked. Trump has spoken out against common core.

The public universities are controlled by the government by virtue of the power of the purse. Universities are funded by government subsidies and the availability of student loans guaranteed by the government. Understandably, the administrators owe their allegiance to a bigger, larger government. The government "thought" police are hard at work outlawing the expression of any opinion that disagrees with theirs at our universities. They are supporting various forms of hate speech while outlawing free speech by others.

Universities are creating "safe zones" that outlaw speech that does not agree with prevailing liberal thought. They refuse to retain speakers for University events unless they have a liberal world view. One University is even providing counseling to students that have been "traumatized" by campaign slogans written in caulk. The list of actions they are taking to suppress speech is almost endless. They have invented a new term, "microaggression", which describes even the slightest perceived offense as aggression. By suppressing speech, they are, by design, suppressing the exchange of ideas. What a mess!

Political correctness enforced by the "speech" police is truly the path to tyranny. One definition of tyranny is - cruel and oppressive government or rule. Isn't this exactly what happened with Obamacare? Passing this bill was an example of speech repression in its most insidious form. The Speaker of the House of Representatives famously said "we have to pass the bill so that you can find out what is in it, away from the fog of controversy". Replace the words "fog of controversy" with "free speech" and you get the idea.

Obamacare was stuffed down the throats of Americans without one congressional vote by a party representing half of the country's people. It was done in the dark recesses of congress, far from the light of day. Opposition was shouted down. People that disagreed with the law were said to be in favor of killing ill people. Details of Obamacare were hidden from the public until after it was passed. Outright lies were told to the public such as "if you like your doctor, you can keep your doctor".

The damage done to Americans has been huge. We have lost our choice of doctor. We have lost our choice of insurance plan. Our money has been appropriated by the government in the form of significantly higher insurance premiums and deductibles. This money is being distributed to special interests chosen by the government. All this happened because a number of professional politicians decided they knew what was best for us. And there was no need for us to talk about it. Just keep quiet and take what we give you.

Another example is climate change. It is being touted as the biggest threat to humanity in our history. The politicians and special interests are constantly stating that "the science is settled" on global warming. In other words, if you disagree with us just shut up and let us distribute your wealth to the global warming special interests. Personally, I don't believe we are even capable of settling the science at this time. Only someone with a God complex would think that they were that smart. I will remind you, in my lifetime, we were convinced that global cooling was the problem.

If you are Christian, freedom to express your religious beliefs is being systematically dismantled. All signs of Christianity are being removed from public property. Expressions of a Christian belief in schools is being eliminated. In the interest of brevity, I will use one simple example to illustrate what the speech/thought police are doing. They are trying, and succeeding, in erasing the term "Merry Christmas" from our country. It is now happy holidays, or winter break or whatever. It is being stricken from the name of parties, store windows and the lexicon of many media outlets. It is portrayed as discriminatory. Slowly, ever so slowly, it is vanishing like the sun setting over the horizon. It would almost make sense not to recognize one particular religion's holiday if it wasn't so ridiculous in this case. The entire purpose of the holiday is to celebrate the birth of Christ. And a big part of the reason this country exists is because Christians wanted to freely celebrate their faith.

Recently, the Washingtonian magazine has taken political correctness to a new level. Their editor has suggested that the term "start a family" is offensive therefore we should not use this term. Apparently the term devalues people who don't have children. Is it children, religion, marriage or something else they hate? I honestly know where to go with this ridiculous line of thought, so I'll just leave it to your imagination.

Politics is rife with people that will shout you down if you express an opinion that differs with theirs. They will play the race card, or the gender card or any of the cards in their deck. If they don't have an appropriate card, they will just call you mean-spirited or other nasty names. All in an attempt to stifle free expression of thought in order to get what they want. The ends justifying the means. The attitude seems to be that, if the facts don't fit, then you must be made to submit. I have never heard Trump seek to divide citizens based on race, residency, gender or any other characteristic for his own personal gain. I have never heard him try to suppress the speech of others. Sometimes he is unkind to the political elites. Sometimes the truth hurts.

Returning People Back to Their Homes

Ted Nugent

Regardless of how outrageous it may sound, let's not lose sight of what Trump is saying. He is saying let's return the people who entered our country illegally back to their own country. He goes on to say that they can then apply to re-enter our country legally. Will this happen if Trump is elected President? It is doubtful that 10,000,000+ people will be returned to their own countries. Is the discussion valid? Absolutely. Will criminals be deported and kept out? You can bet on it. As a resident of a border, "invasion state", I certainly hope the criminals are kicked out and kept out. So why is Trump so focused on illegal immigration?

This is, by far, the most difficult campaign issue to write about. It is packed with philosophical, spiritual and moral, almost unanswerable, questions. There are two key core components of the "illegal" immigration question. Who has the right to be inside American borders? Secondly, what do the people "legally" inside the borders owe, or want to give to those who decide to enter "illegally". This is not a race issue; it is an illegal vs. legal issue.

The question of who has the right to be on American soil seems pretty clear when viewed in the context of international norms. The citizens of the land encompassed by the borders of the United States have the recognized right to decide who can enter the country. There may be philosophic questions as to who really owns the land anyway. Aren't we just stewards of the land to be passed on to the next generations? Who was here first? For the most part, it doesn't really matter. For purposes of this election it is what it is. To argue against international norms about borders would invite wars and chaos. Trump seems pretty clear on what he believes.

The question of who we want to let in is personal. Like it or not, this country was founded and prospered under a Judeo-Christian value system. These values include love of thy neighbor and helping the less fortunate. As a result, America has been the most charitable country in the history of the world. But this question is not easy to answer without factoring in the economic and societal implications. I choose to believe that most people are good and that Americans want to help as many people as much as they can. Unfortunately, our illegal immigration policies seem to have been driven by politicians and special interests. You can tell who they are since they are the ones shouting "racists" and "bigots" at anyone who would interfere with their votes or interests.

The ability to help others needs to be taken in context. In family terms, our American family is spending more than we make. Significantly more. We are borrowing and spending nearly $1 trillion dollars a year. We are up to our ears in debt. In reality, we have no extra money for anything, we have no savings. We don't even have a single dime saved to pay future Social Security benefits for our own citizens. We can't even afford to supply clean water to the residents of Flint, Michigan. Any incremental money we spend needs to be borrowed. There is always a limit to how much anyone can borrow. There has always been a limit to how long a debtor nation can remain solvent. If a country is not solvent, then its citizens can expect a dramatic reduction in lifestyle. If our entire financial system collapses, we will not be in a position to help anyone.

For years many special interests have tacitly supported illegal immigration in order for big businesses to have a supply of "cheap labor". Others have viewed them as a source of votes. In invasion states, it is not too difficult to vote if you are not a citizen. When you hear a politician say "voting rights" it is code for making it easier for non-citizens to vote. There are also people who want to help those in need. So there are a number of explanations why there are **at least** 10,000,000 people residing in our country illegally. And these reasons are not mutually exclusive.

Unquestionably, the primary motivation for illegal immigration is economic. Politicians will say - they just want to get a job, and work hard at jobs Americans don't want to do in order to support their families. That may be so, but it has repercussions for our legal citizens. In areas where illegal immigrants are allowed to work on the cheap, Americans find it harder to get jobs. This was true in my state until a law was passed requiring employers to obtain proof of citizenship in order to hire an employee. There are also those who say - they pay taxes that make up for their cost to our society. Our generous benefits cannot possibly be supported by the low wages earned by the percentage of illegal immigrants that actually do have a tax-paying job. A large percentage of illegal workers are paid "under-the-table", therefore they don't pay any taxes. And much of what they take from us is sent back to their native countries.

The cost to citizens of educating and supporting illegal immigrants who live off governmental support is beyond calculation. It undoubtedly costs well over one hundred billion dollars each year. The aid programs that are available to them range from free health care to food stamps to aid for dependent children to rent subsidies and on and on. In many cases our governments have chosen to allow easy access to these programs, even to non-citizens. The people here illegally know how to access these programs. It is obvious to anyone that uses a hospital emergency room in an invasion state. It would be unreasonable to assume that there wasn't a fair amount of fraud involved as well. As an example, some people claim that they have more children than they actually have, thereby increasing the aid they receive.

Just this month the Obama administration said they were budgeting $1.3 billion for just 75,000 "minors" he has encouraged to come here from Central America. That is roughly $17,600 per "minor". The average social security for our citizens who have worked their entire life is $14,800. Stunning isn't it! And this $1.3 billion is just a tiny, tiny, fraction of what illegal immigration costs us.

If you think all of this doesn't affect you, stay tuned as they move to your state. Ask a person living in an invasion state what is happening in their public schools. Resources are being shifted to educate the millions of illegal immigrants. Just to give you a low-ball idea, just $15,000 a year to educate each of two million illegal kids would be $30 billion a year. And I am way understating the number of students and cost per student. Class sizes are increasing, electives like art and music are being eliminated, classes for gifted children are being eliminated as resources are poured into English as a second language(ESL). Teaching is being dumbed down so that no one will be left behind.

A big deal was made of Trump's comment on illegals being rapists and murderers. Taken literally it was quite shocking. However only a fool would suggest he meant all of them. How many there are as a percentage of the population is not the issue. But we do know that not an insignificant number are criminals, probably hundreds of thousands. According to government statistics, Obama decided not to deport, but instead proudly released 19,732 illegals from our prisons to roam freely among American citizens during 2015 alone. These criminals averaged 3-25 convictions each. They consisted of 8,234 violent crimes including 208 murders and 900 sex crimes. This number is about half of prior years' 30-40 thousand released only because our government has made a political decision to stop arresting so many illegals that commit crimes. Keep in mind, these are only the convicted numbers, the criminals that are never tried and convicted are in addition to these.

In the days before political correctness you would have heard on the news about many more illegals committing crimes. In border states, over half of reported burglaries are committed by illegals. Our current administration currently employs a fishing strategy when dealing with illegal immigrant criminals. It's called - catch and release. The only difference is that they ask the released fish to swim back for trial. Want to guess how many come swimming back? So we would guess virtually all of the catch and release criminals are still on the streets of America.

In any case it is obvious to anyone who wants to see that there are quite a few violent criminals among the illegal immigrants. Many cites have even created safe (sanctuary) zones to protect these criminals from the law. Why would cities have set up all these safe zones if there were no criminals to protect? How many as a percentage of the population is not the issue. You can take it to the bank that most Americans don't want any non-citizen criminals in this country. Only someone with motives contrary to the safety of American citizens would support imported crime. That is Trump's point, he will not tolerate criminals who are not even citizens.

Then there is the question of drug gangs. Anyone can go onto the internet and see videos of heavily armed men running backpacks of drugs around our southern borders. Illegal immigrants reputedly control large parts of the drug trade in our country. These people are vicious and violent people. We house at lease 100,000 of them in our prisons at the cost of at least $2 billion per year. The media would have you believe that all the recent legal immigrants welcome the flood of illegal immigrants. Nothing could be further from the truth. The immigrants in this country, legally, don't want the criminals here either since they are the most likely to be victimized by crime and school overcrowding.

It is generally accepted that immigration has been a key factor in our success as a nation. The diversity and energy created by immigrants is undeniable. But only when the immigrants integrated into our society. Closed societies do not fare as well. A modern example is the country of Japan, which is now in a state of decline partially due to their racially closed society. On the other hand, our system of robust and fair laws, along with the enforcement of those laws, has also been important to our nation. No laws, no nation.

Illegal immigration also poses a structural danger to our society. For 200 years the American way of life has prospered under the concept of the melting pot. Peoples of all languages and cultures would assimilate into our society by learning English and adapting our way of life. Most importantly they would take pride in their new country. That has all changed. We now see immigrants waving Mexican flags and burning American flags during "protests". We have become a decidedly bi-lingual society. Illegal immigrants are almost encouraged to speak their own native language, and to owe their allegiance to their home country. They can vote, receive benefits, be taught in our schools and get a driver's license, all without knowing a word of English. There are huge areas of invasion cities where not a word of English can be seen or heard spoken. As a result, we have become a politically, socially and economically fractured society. I can't think of a society in the history of the world that has prospered by fostering a culturally fractured society. Obama would have you believe it to be true, but he never gives an example of where a fractured culture has made a country stronger.

The key "right" that can be exercised using Spanish is voting. Logically if people could only vote in English, there would be no incentive for politicians to enable the fracturing of our society. Many politicians also work tirelessly to end any identification procedure for a person to vote. They do this under the guise of not excluding legally entitled citizens of their right to vote. This is obviously not an honest explanation for why they don't want to require identification to be part of the voting process. All citizens have numerous documents to establish their identification. You can't even get on a plane or cash a check without identification as examples. It is widely thought that many people in this country illegally do vote. If this is true, then that could be a key reason many politicians tirelessly encourage illegal immigration.

Until Trump brashly spoke out about illegal immigration, we have been blindly traveling down a road to economic and societal destruction. It has become politically incorrect to speak your opinion about illegal immigration if you oppose it. The federal government has decided that they will selectively not enforce immigration laws. Various state and local governments have decided to turn a blind eye to enforcement of criminal laws broken by illegal immigrants. We have been incurring billions upon billions of debt to pay the enormous costs of supporting illegal immigrants. These are death spiral issues that will not resolve themselves. Trump exercised his right of free speech and yanked our heads out of the sand. He is empowering people of all opinions to express their opinions. He clearly states where he stands. He wants to control our borders. He wants to return people illegally in our country back to their own country. He wants to have people come back to our country legally. He wants to enforce our laws, including a zero tolerance policy toward criminal illegal immigrants.

Can Radical Islamist Terrorism Be Stopped?

"All that is necessary for the triumph
of evil is that good men do nothing"

Edmund Burke

More than 1.5 billion people identify themselves as Muslims. This amounts to roughly one out of every four people on earth. They inhabit virtually every part of the world. What they believe, I have no idea. My reason in broaching the subject is the spread of terrorism by people identifying themselves as Muslims. Whether you choose to call them Radical Islamic Terrorists or just plain terrorists, their actions have the same impact on their victims. Dead is dead. Somewhere between 5% and 30% of Muslims support the terrorists. Quick math tells me that just 5% of 1.5 billion is 75,000,000 people. Not a small number.

Parts of the world have been under attack by this form of terrorism for over 1,000 years. Starting in the Middle East and spreading to southern Europe and India. Eventually reaching Asia and our own shores. The brutality they have inflicted on people is horrendous. I don't believe there is much dispute in America that it should be stopped.

We had our first battles with them soon after our

country was founded. Muslim pirates from the north coast of Africa attacked our merchant ships in order to loot them and enslave Christians. With hardly a navy to speak of, Thomas Jefferson attacked them in 1801 until they finally decided that messing with us wasn't worth their trouble. Apparently, they once again feel it is worthwhile to attack us. It is no wonder, since we send them weapons through their proxy states, while refusing to arm the Kurds and Jordanians that are fighting against them. We have a president that has said the Muslim call to prayer is the sweetest sound he has ever heard. We have destabilized many of the countries in the Middle East. Of course they feel emboldened. So what has Trump said we should do?

Trump has talked about cutting off the lifeblood of terrorism, money. He has said we should take their oil which is a primary source of their money. He has also said we should prohibit banks from dealing with terrorists. Cut off their money and you restrict their ability to sustain their activities. He has also said "bomb the hell out of them". Our air-power has almost unlimited ability to thwart their territorial control. It may not appear to be effective but that is only because our current administration has severely restricted our military activities. He has not suggested lots of boots on the ground. A thousand years of history has demonstrated that it just doesn't work. His philosophy appears to be that we should do what we need to do with the least cost and loss of American military lives.

Trump has been criticized for saying he would cut off the terrorists' access to the internet. They have used the internet effectively for recruiting and attack planning. Quite frankly, he doesn't seem to give a darn about their right to free speech if it is used to kill us. He is putting our safety first, over political correctness and the special interests of the internet companies. He has also said that he will not stand by while they slaughter Christians.

What Trump has not done is continue the mantra that Islam is a peace loving religion. How would he know if it is? It seems reasonable that he refrains from repeating the mantra if the religious leaders of Islam themselves are not shouting it from the rooftops, or aggressively leading the fight against the terrorists.

Trump has also expressed the attitude that our safety is paramount. He has proposed temporarily denying entry into our country for certain Muslims until we can get a handle on the situation. He has also proposed building a wall on the southern border to cut off this avenue of access for terrorists. He is also against the efforts by our current administration to bring in untold tens of thousands of "refugees" (including many military aged men) from the Middle East which is part of Obama's effort to Islamize our society. He is putting our safety before political correctness. Europe has put political correctness before safety and it is a mess. Pockets of cities are now governed by Sharia law. Rapes of women and terrorist activities are rampant. I have canceled a trip to Paris for that very reason. I like Trump's priorities better than Europe's.

Political correctness has hampered our efforts to stop terrorists by not allowing us to profile them. The following is a personal experience with profiling before political correctness became more important than our safety. When I was 18 I decided to take time off from school after graduating from high school. I looked like a typical hippie. I was young, had long hair and dressed the part, headband and all. Around that time there had been a rash of airplane hijackings. I had a plane change in Chicago during a cross country flight. While waiting for my next plane, I was approached by two suits with badges who asked to speak to me. I accompanied them to a small windowless room where they then proceeded to shake me down. When they were satisfied I was not a threat they turned me loose. I asked them why they had chosen me. They informed me that I fit the profile of a hijacker. I wasn't happy, but neither was I insulted. I didn't want to be hijacked any more than the next guy.

Fast forward to 2002 when my family was inside the Orlando airport. My 9-year-old son was selected to be searched under enhanced security measures due to 9/11. Meanwhile, men of all ages and cultures walked right on through. I remember thinking at the time that we could not be serious if this was our answer to thwarting terrorist attacks. One thing I feel certain about is that Trump will not put political correctness ahead of my safety.

We have experienced dozens of terrorist attacks in our country. Most have been labeled as something else in order to maintain the charade that we are not in danger from Muslim terrorists. The government and media could not cover up the recent murders committed by Muslim terrorists in San Bernardino. At least one neighbor of the terrorists had known something unusual was going on at the terrorists' house. But they had not notified anyone of their suspicions for fear of being called a racist. Political correctness at work! Almost unbelievably, military style equipment, used to respond to just such attacks, was being pulled out of Oakland that very same week. Again, for political correctness reasons. Our current administration has been aggressively removing military style equipment from our cities because they think it just doesn't look politically correct. If you think political correctness can't kill us, think again.

An Experienced Executive

"First they ignore you, then they
laugh at you, then they fight you,
then you win"

Mahatma Gandhi

Yippee! That is a one-word answer to those who
knock Trump for not having experience as a
professional politician. We have elected to the
presidency one professional politician after another.
Do you feel better off because of it? Trump would
tell you that professional politicians are a big reason
we are in the mess we are in. We've elected
professional politicians for decades, how's that
working out for you? One definition of "insanity" is
continuing to do the same thing over and over but
expecting a different result. Isn't that what we have
been doing? Trump is shouting - stop the madness!
And people are listening. Americans may be crazy
but most of us aren't insane. So yes, when people
scream that Trump has no experience as a
professional politician, a lot of people are shouting -
Yippee!

The following reflects what I believe to be a simple
example of the difference between a professional
politician and a person who desires to serve our
country. When the Power-Ball lottery recently
reached the fantastic sum of $1.5 billion dollars it
garnered enormous attention. Trump was asked
what he would do with the money if he won. He
immediately replied that he would give it to our

veterans. Hillary Clinton was asked the same question. It took her a while to come up with a worthwhile cause but ultimately she said that she would fund her campaign. One person is a professional politician, one is not. I'm not sure what else to say about that. Some people are generous with your money and others are generous with theirs. "For where your treasure is, there your heart will be also", Luke 12:34.

So what is Trump if he is not an "experienced" politician? He is a person who took what he had and turned it into a wildly successful multi-billion-dollar international enterprise. Critics will say that Trump had an advantage because his family had money therefore he had a great education and the other perks of being born into a wealthy family. Hard to argue with that. There is a baseball saying for people who had such an advantage and rest on their laurels - he was born on third base and thought he hit a triple. Trump may have been born on third base but he didn't just stand on third base and rest on his laurels. He kept coming back to the plate and hit home-run after home-run. That is taking your God given talents and making the most of them. By his own calculations he is worth billions of dollars.

Trump is the Chief Executive Officer(CEO) of a vast array of successful enterprises. That means he is the person vested with the ultimate responsibility for the success or failure of the organization. That is just about as close as you can get to the definition of the President of the United States. When we elect a president, we in effect hire a President. In the non-governmental world people aren't hired for positions because they really, really want to be. They are hired primarily because of their ability to do the job. Americans have gotten into the habit of hiring (electing) people based on how bad they want it, their ability to raise money and to make good speeches. As an example, no large non-governmental enterprise in the world would hire a person whose main accomplish was "community organizing" to be their CEO. We just did that, twice, to run our country! Now, as Trump would say, we have a mess.

Our government is the vastest man-made organization on the planet earth. We need someone who can process the enormous complexities of our government. We need someone who can juggle activities related to our military, congress, the media, foreign leaders, the needs of our citizens and much more. That person should also be able to make agreements requiring compromises with various parties that may not see eye to eye with each other. We need a person that can hire competent employees, inspire them and lead them to success. We need a person who can communicate effectively with us and people around the world. Many of us want a president that will build on what we have and make America greater that what it already is. Our president should have strong Judeo-Christian values, even if they are not a Christian, unless we chose to scrap all that has made us great and start over. Although this is a partial list you get the idea.

There are also important character qualifications in being a president. On top of the list are trustworthiness and honesty. A CEO/President's actions filter throughout an entire organization. If they are dishonest or not trustworthy then everyone in the organization will feel free to follow their example. We have historically been a transparent nation of laws and open government. The president has the responsibility for the enforcement of our laws. This is not to be confused with making our laws. That is clearly the responsibility of congress. Consider if we elected a president that was not honest or trustworthy. The president and his employees would feel free to lie to us and cover-up their activities. They would also feel free to ignore the enforcement of laws they didn't agree with. They would also feel free to apply their own interpretation to laws and punitively enforce them against people they didn't like. They could lie to congress about their actions. Kind of scary huh? Sound familiar?

Let's take a hypothetical example that I'm sure everyone can relate to, the IRS. Say for example we had an administration that played by their own rules. Say they didn't like one particular group of citizens that were political rivals and the IRS employees felt empowered to treat that group unfairly. Well, no problem, you would say. We would simply have the appropriate regulators investigate these unfair practices and then discipline any employees who had applied the laws unjustly. Ah, but what if we had a president that agreed with these unlawful actions. What if the employees destroyed evidence of wrongdoing such as computer storage devices? What if the offending employees were not disciplined? What if the employees lied to regulators and congress about their actions? Imagine if you took this hypothetical example and multiplied it by a million actions by our government employees. Even imagine if we had partisan Cabinet Members who decided they could hide or destroy their correspondence or emails to keep their activities hidden. Kind of chilling isn't it?

If our standard for president was perfection, there wouldn't be any viable candidates. How does Trump stack up on honesty and trustworthiness?   I have never met the man therefore I can only go by what his actions have displayed. Vetted is a popular word in "media-speak". Vetting is the process of performing a background check on someone before offering them employment. How well has Trump been vetted? As outlined below, Trump has had very significant business activities throughout the world.

In order to accomplish his business objectives, he would have had to be in compliance with hundreds of thousands, if not millions, of laws and regulations. He would have had to work with thousands and thousands of regulating agencies throughout the world regarding building codes, environmental, safety, financial stability and a myriad of such issues. He would have had to file millions of pages of documents to various agencies. It gives me a headache just thinking about it! He would have had untold numbers of loan agreements and disclosures to banks throughout the world. Banks may be the most highly regulated corporate entities in the world. In essence, if he is dealing with them he is also subject to be being reviewed by the banks' regulators. His activities would be scrutinized by other parties he would deal with. A partial list would include unions, utilities and civil rights groups. I doubt there could be a more stringent vetting process than he has experienced in his business activities. He has done all of this successfully. If he were a crook or a liar he surely would have been outed as such, particularly given his high profile in the media. Well, he is still standing!

There is the issue of several bankruptcies involving a casino bearing his name. This was not a personal bankruptcy. Trump did not ever file for personal bankruptcy as some of his detractors would have you believe. It is beyond the scope of this book to get into all the details. That would require an entire book to describe. Bankruptcy is part of the legal structure in our country. If done in the proper manner it is a legal personal and business activity. Bankruptcy in our country has been viewed as a necessary part of our legal system. Centuries ago in England people who could not pay their debts were thrown into "debtors prisons" until they could pay. As you can imagine, not many debtors paid their debts from prison.

We as a country have decided that is appropriate to have an option for people and corporations to file bankruptcy. Imagine if you could, if the millions of people in this country who have filed for bankruptcy were rotting away in prisons until they could repay their debts. Doesn't sound like a very workable system. To be clear many innocent people are harmed by a bankruptcy. But that doesn't make people who file for bankruptcy immoral or criminals. It is neither rare nor unusual for people or corporations to file for bankruptcy. Trump has had a handful of his organizations file for bankruptcy out of probably thousands he has controlled. What would you expect him to do, voluntarily show up at the door of a prison? He has endured times where he has struggled financially but has bounced back stronger than ever. Isn't that what our country needs right now?

So, is Trump qualified to be president? What has he actually done to demonstrate that he is capable of being the most important CEO in the world? Trump has built or controlled skyscrapers all over the world including New York City, Chicago, Vancouver, Florida, Istanbul, Dubai, Brazil, Uruguay, and the Philippines to name some. He controls a portfolio of golf courses in the U.S., the U.K. and Dubai. He has built a media empire that includes TV shows such as The Apprentice and beauty pageants. He manages an ice skating rink in Central Park, NYC. He has written over a dozen successful books. He has a merchandise portfolio that includes clothing among other items. I am sure I have missed some of his accomplishments but you get the idea. His list of business accomplishments rivals anything I have ever seen considering its size, diversity of activities and geographical reach. It is also important to recognize he has done this profitably. What does this say about Trump's ability to manage a complex organization such as the U.S. Government? His accomplishments clearly indicate he is qualified beyond a reasonable doubt.

Anyone who thinks government can do most things better than private enterprises just isn't paying attention. If you need proof, walk over to your bill file and grab your medical insurance bill. How does it compare to before Obama took over the health-care industry? A lot higher now, isn't it? How are the airport TSA security lines working out for you? I could go on for pages, but you get the idea. I would rather have a cost-effective business solution to our problems than a wasteful government program. Trump would hire the best people to do the job we need done efficiently and at the lowest cost possible.

A Pragmatic, Adaptable, Executive

"There are two kinds of fools: Those who can't change their opinions and those who won't."

Josh Billings

One of the criticisms leveled at Trump is the fact that he has changed his mind on some issues over the years. He has also changed his political party. I can't believe one single American has never changed their opinion on many things over their lifetime. In fact, we are known as an adaptable culture. Adaptability is one of the attributes that has made our country great.

I started life as a democrat, then I was a republican and now I am neither. I don't feel the need to apologize. I was a democrat at 18 for practical reasons. The city I lived in was controlled by the democrats. When my older brother registered as a republican our property taxes promptly went up. From then on we were all democrats and our taxes went back down. I became a republican because they were fiscally conservative. When they stopped being fiscally conservative I dumped them also. Real life choices made by one person. Doesn't any candidate face the same choices?

Changing your beliefs is not the same as changing what you say. It is not the same as "I was for it before I was against it" as in the case of the Iraq war. If you are now against war and that is why you changed your mind, fine. If you still believe in interventionist wars and nation building, then that is different. You have simply realized that in the case of that particular war it didn't work out so it was a mistake. You are simply admitting you made a mistake in that particular case. Trump was originally against that war because he didn't believe it was the right thing to do. He still feels that way.

People change their minds for all kinds of reasons. The advancement of science, personal experiences, growing older and dramatic life events are a few of the reasons. Some people say early in life that they don't want to have children. Yet as they age they change their minds. Someone might have wanted a bigger, more expensive house. Yet after the housing bubble they may never want it. A person may have believed in an aggressive foreign policy. Maybe they lose a loved one in a war and change their mind. Someone may have believed that a certain disease could spread by touch. But then after medical science evolved they knew it was not true.

Trump has been criticized for changing his views on abortion. He has said his change of opinion was due to a personal experience. Who can judge what is in a person's heart? Only their speech and actions provide but an imperfect window. Consistency from the moment of change is a "tell" as they say in poker. Professional politicians have become adept at playing to the crowd. They say one thing to a crowd in one state and a different thing to a crowd in another state. That is not a change in opinion, it is deception. They may change their stated beliefs based on opinion polls, not on what they believe. That is not a personal opinion change. That is an expedient action in an effort to get votes. Pundits call it flip-flopping. Once again, who can say which is which? Trump has appeared to me as a normal person who has changed some of his opinions over time.

The pundits are pounding Trump to give them details of everything he will do if elected. When a large company needs a new CEO to run the company, the Board of Directors has the responsibility to make that decision. When we vote for president, we are hiring a person to lead our country. Boards don't ask a CEO candidate to give them a list of all the decisions that they will make over the next four years. Any Board of Directors understands that the world is a very fluid and dynamic environment. Our country will be better served by a president that will make decisions based on the conditions existing at the time, not based on a canned campaign promise list detailing every decision he will make.

Conservatives are not happy that Trump has expressed willingness to work with liberals in the congress. Liberals have obviously also not wanted to work with conservatives as they have reelected a president that has demonstrated disdain for anyone that doesn't agree with him. All I can say to them is - get real. There simply aren't that many non-negotiable issues facing our country.

During recent presidential elections, Americans

have been virtually evenly split between a "conservative" and a "liberal" candidate. No one side is ever going to get exactly what they want unless it is forced upon the other half that don't agree with them, as was the case with Obamacare. That is not America. Taken to an extreme, it is more like Iraq where the portion of the population in control suppresses the opposition. First under Saddam, and then under the Iranian controlled leaders, different groups have suppressed the others in Iraq. The result has been poverty, and unimaginable bloodshed.

The icon of modern conservatives, Ronald Reagan, was known for his ability to work effectively with members of the opposition party. He acted as if he was president of all Americans, not just those that agreed with him. He spoke in terms of uniting us. He did not denigrate people simply because they had a different view than him. He was reelected in a landslide. His victory demonstrated that we are Americans first, not republicans or democrats. Trump has said unkind things about some of our politicians. I can't say that most of us agree with his approach. But if you listen carefully he does not insult people for what they believe. He attacks them for the way they have acted. That is a big difference if you hope to unite a country.

A strong economy and military make all other things possible. They are non-negotiable. Without these we are simply rearranging the deck chairs on the Titanic. Trump has emphasized both of these pillars of our great nation.   On other matters he will have his opinions but will negotiate about how to achieve these goals as he has done in business his entire life. We negotiate continually in our everyday lives. When we negotiate, we are compromising. When we buy a car we negotiate a price that both a seller and a buyer will agree to. Both parties would want a different price but agree to compromise. That is how the world works. Trump has a reputation as a master negotiator. What Trump has said is that he will negotiate good deals with those who disagree with him. I believe that is where conservatives have missed his point.

Conservative voters have been angry not because of compromises but rather because there has been little compromise. The professional politicians elected by conservatives have not used their positions to effectively represent their voters. Too often they have simply gotten what they personally needed. They have represented their special interest donors that they need to keep happy in order to get reelected.

The latest budget bill is representative of the "get what I need" mentality. It was passed by funding virtually everything. Significant changes were not made to cut waste or unnecessary spending. Conservatives did not even cut off government support for organizations that harvest baby parts for sale. There was no compromise, it was essentially - let's just spend everything all the politicians need to please their special interest groups. The negotiating was over who got how much. Everyone goes home happy and we continue to spiral into debt. Champaign corks pop all over Washington D.C. and we get the bill. Conservatives may have negotiated but they did not get a good deal for the people who elected them.

This is not just a conservative issue. Millions of liberals have been greatly harmed by the non-negotiated Obamacare law as an example. Liberals have also lost their choice of doctors and seen their medical costs soar as a result of a few people getting what they want with no regard to the majority of Americans. As the medical costs soar for our nation, our economy weakens. Trump would want to negotiate a deal that would provide medical care for all Americans in an effective and efficient manner. Not in a job-killing, economically destructive, manner that causes financial pain for hundreds of millions of Americans.

It is important that we judge the president's ability to effectively make deals and compromises that are in the best interest of the vast majority of Americans. We need someone who has demonstrated the ability to work effectively with people holding different views. Not just domestically, but internationally as well. Most politicians fall into one of two categories. Worn out professional politicians that have thrived in the currently divisive system or those that have not been effective in bringing about meaningful positive change. Trump is neither of these. He is a demonstrably successful negotiator. He could not have achieved what he has without the ability to get along with all types of people. More importantly, he has not been bought and paid for by special interest donors.

Fair Trade, not Free Trade

"The world's a mean place, It's unfair,
then it's fair. It's hateful, then it's
loving. It's a very peculiar place on
philosophical and metaphysical and
religious levels."

Tim Allen

Trump has spoken quite a bit about China so I will focus on this particular country. How are we doing in our trade with China? China sells over $300-500 billion dollars more of products to us every year than we sell to them. Not so good. It has been estimated we have lost 3,000,000-5,000,000 jobs as a result of trading with China alone. And this number would probably vastly understate the jobs we lost. As a result of our trade with China we now owe them over $1.2 trillion dollars! We trade our future for their cheap labor. Sounds fair to me. Make no mistake, the special interests have created this imbalance. Large U.S. companies love the cheap labor. Banks make fortunes off the loans to finance this trade. Our business leaders would love to make the products and create jobs here but they can't afford to under our corrupt system.

Our trade agreements are negotiated in the private, expensive meetings and dinners attended by our professional politicians. Not to worry, of courses the politicians consult with their large donors to make sure we get a fair deal. The professional politicians are hard at work on their latest sell out of American workers. It's called the Trans-Pacific Partnership(TTP). It is being negotiated in secret, not unlike Obamacare, and we know how that worked out. Our prior Secretary of State, Mrs. Clinton, even made the TTP deal a high priority, although that may have changed now with votes on the line. That is how it works, I love it for the contributions but no wait, I'm not so sure about it with workers' votes on the line. Never mind, just elect me and I'll work it out in private.

Meanwhile, China blocks U.S. companies at every turn from selling our products into their country. Ask anyone who tries to sell products into China. Our government will tell you, sure but, we sell billions worth of products to China. This is true, but much of what we sell to China is repackaged and sold right back to us. China pirates our technology and hacks our computers. There have even been stores in China that look exactly like Apple stores but are entirely counterfeit right down to the Logos. Our government response is similar to a pet dog that rolls over on its back expecting to be scratched. That a boy.

So why is labor cheaper in China? Let's start with the workers. They are barely paid subsistence wages. They are packed in living quarters like rats. They include young children. They have working conditions reminiscent of the brutal conditions in a Victorian era Dickens novel. If they complain they can be replaced in a heartbeat by any of millions of others waiting to get a job. Although this is not true of all Chinese manufacturers it is true enough for too many to ignore.

I have belonged to six unions in my life. Why any union worker, not employed by the government, would vote for anyone but Trump is beyond me. Politicians of both parties have been killing jobs in this country for decades in the name of free trade. And the jobs we have lost have been replaced by workers in other countries under working conditions contrary to everything unions represent. In addition, wages for union and non-union workers in America have been driven down in a quest to compete with cheap foreign labor. American workers can barely eke out a living.

How about the environment that we care so deeply about? What is this "free trade" doing to the environment of the world? The air in the capital city of China, Beijing, is so polluted you practically need to wear night vision glasses in the middle of the day just to see. But have no fear. Obama negotiated a global warming deal with China to solve this problem. Interestingly, on the very day Chinese officials were bragging about meeting Obama's goals they had to shut down activity in Beijing because the air pollution was so high. Meanwhile back at home, jobs are being lost to hold up our part of the deal. Their water is unsafe to drink in many areas of the country. It has been estimated that over 70% of rivers and lakes in China are polluted by industrial activities. But you get the idea. Our jobs are being sent to other countries that don't have to follow our environmental laws. Our environmental laws add a significant cost to business activity in this country. We have decided that regulations are important, but only in this country.

We have extensive product safety laws in this

country. These range from food ingredients to physical products such as baby strollers. It is cheaper to make virtually everything we consume or utilize in our daily lives if safety is not a concern. It can be cheaper if ingredients or materials used are unsafe or substandard. It is cheaper if products are cheaply designed. As high as 50% of the products recalled in America were imported from China. These range from toothpaste to lead covered toys to dog food. The dog food issue is particularly troubling. How are dogs expected to protect themselves? I have been forced to carefully scrutinize dog food to make sure that they are not made in China using dangerous chemicals. And it is not easy to determine where a product is really made. You have to carefully search the fine print on the labels. Even so, country of origin can be cleverly disguised.

In the case of food and product safety our government does try to monitor imports for violations of our safety laws. Unfortunately, it is a daunting task to completely protect us against producers that intentionally subvert our laws. In this country executives that intentionally subverted our safety laws would go to jail. In China they would buy another Porsche.

Chinese companies are showered with government loans. Many of these loans would never be made if they were expected to be paid back. But the goal of government loans in China appears to be the creation of jobs rather than the return of the money loaned. In essence, these loans represent free money used to produce products for export thereby creating Chinese jobs. They have also kept their currency below it's true value. These policies put products manufactured in the U.S. at a competitive cost disadvantage. Goodbye jobs. Of course our companies get some financing assistance from our government as well but this assistance pales in comparison to Chinese financing subsidies. With help from their government, Chinese companies are now borrowing record amounts of money. The money they are borrowing is being used to pay down older debt. China has created a debt bubble that will make our housing bubble look like a picnic in the park when it explodes. And our Federal Reserve has enabled this situation with their free money policies. Trump has often spoken out against China's unfair trade practices and currency manipulation.

I agree with Trump that the Chinese are good people. They are simply doing what they allowed to do by their government, and ours, to make a living. In fact, more millionaires are being created in China than anywhere else in the world. They are obviously very talented. There have been many positive results from our trade with China but they have come at a cost. They have systematically accumulated billions of wealth every year at our expense. International trade is a very important part of our daily lives. But as Trump has said, it needs to be fair. Currently "free trade" is nothing but a sell-out of American citizens.

Trump is not an isolationist. He has built many projects in countries all over the world. He obviously appreciates international trade and feels comfortable dealing with foreign citizens and countries. I have no doubt Trump would work hard to even the playing field for American workers while providing opportunities for foreign interests. If elected using no special interest money, he would owe nothing to anyone but the American people. He is a master negotiator and even wrote a bestselling book - The Art of the Deal. In the book he talks about a key part of fair agreements being the courage to walk away from a bad deal. As president, I have no doubt he would walk away from any deal that was bad for the American public. That is how he has operated his entire successful career. In any case, it is hard to imagine he could do worse than what we have now.

Trump's Foreign Policy

"Those who do not remember the
past are condemned to repeat it."

George Santayana

Trump's foreign policy is quite simple - America first.
He will do what is best for our country, but not by
military aggression toward other countries. He will
not surrender our country to globalism. He will be a
loyal friend and a feared enemy. He will not engage
in "nation building". He will insist that other countries
pay their fair share for their defense. He will
strengthen our military. If we have to fight, we will
only fight to win. Radical Islamic terrorist will be hit
hard. In other words, he will do what any sane
person that loved their country would do.

You may have heard pundits asking - do we really
want Trump's finger on the nuclear button? They
kind of wink and chuckle as if to say - you all know
we really need an experienced professional in
charge. The following are some of the major foreign
policy challenges managed by our experienced
professionals over the last 16 years.

History will show that we have made two critical
foreign policy blunders of historic proportions during
the last 16 years. That is two full terms by two
politician presidents. These presidents were
different in many ways but similar in the most fateful

ways. Neither understood history, or the costs and consequences of their actions. The first blunder, committed by President Bush, was attacking Iraq. The second blunder, committed by President Obama, was rushing out of Iraq and leaving a murderous Iranian puppet in charge. Both these decisions were made by experienced politicians and their advisers. Donald Trump spoke out against both actions.

The Middle East has been a powder-keg for centuries. During the entire period of recorded history, the Middle East has been mired in regional wars. Iran and Iraq lost millions of solders fighting each other just a few decades ago. The glue that held the keg together were strong regional leaders who counter-balanced each other while controlling their restless and impoverished citizens. They became "made-up" Nations to begin with. People with different cultures, languages, religions, and allegiances thrown together by western bureaucrats playing with maps after wars that they had won. Neither president seemed to have understood this basic history. Their decisions were a breathtaking display of naivety.

The decision to invade Iraq was made during a time when we had suffered a horrendous terrorist attack by radical Muslims. Undoubtedly, emotions played some part in that decision. That is understandable. According to the official reason out of Washington, we went into Iraq because they had weapons of mass destruction (WMDs). This turned out to be faulty, we found no WMDs. Once again these decisions were based on the opinions of "experts". I think we all realize the pain, suffering and loss of life that has occurred as a result. The estimated cost will probably exceed $3 trillion by the time all the costs are incurred.

The decision to pack up and high-tail it out of Iraq must have been a purely political decision. I refuse to believe we could have elected a president who would be so naive as to believe things would work out if we left a vast oil rich territory, inhabited by armed gangs, with no one in real control. Obama promised to pull out of Iraq and he did. He left the keys with a puppet dictator who was handpicked by the rulers of Iran. A fateful mistake was made to keep an election promise that was made years earlier. The result is a brutal Iraqi government that is supported by tens of billions of our dollars. They are committing thousands of atrocious crimes and murders against their own people. In fact, the people of Iraq voted to democratically change this government and the Obama administration decided they liked the murderous Iranian puppet Maliki better, so we kept him in control. So much for supporting democracy.

Management 101 would teach anyone that when circumstances change, actions should change. Unfortunately, we had a community activist as president. The administration claimed Iraq did not want us there so we had no choice but to leave. At the same time, we send them tens of billions of dollars to use as they wish. It seems logical that had we told them - no U.S. airbase, no money - that we would have had an airbase. Had we had an airbase in Iraq, ISIS would have been wiped out in a New York minute as the Donald might say. Instead we have created an environment in which ISIS can thrive. But not to worry they are only a "J.V. team" according to our president.

Apparently we liked the results of our government overthrow in Iraq so much we decided to expand our efforts. Our administration encouraged the "Arab Spring". It should have been called the "Arab Hell". We encouraged the overthrow of leaders in countries such as Egypt and Libya to name just two. Terror now reigns in these countries. Almost uncountable numbers of their citizens are being tortured and murdered on a daily basis. People who wish harm to the rest of the world are growing more and more powerful every day. No small part of the blame rests with the western powers' intervention into a relativity stable Middle East, turning it into the wild, wild west. For our part, we have an administration filled with political operatives that see the world as they want to see it, rather than as it truly is. They ignore history and reality. They are like a bunch of children blissfully playing in a sand box full of fire ants. I haven't even mentioned Africa where Boko Haram extremists recently killed 86 people in Nigeria, including children burned to death. The 6-year Islamic uprising has killed over 20,000 people and left 2,500,000 people homeless in Nigeria alone.

It would be difficult to ignore the death of four Americans in Benghazi when thinking about who would make a good president. Four people, employed by the U.S. government, were brutally murdered on foreign soil at an American facility. They were stranded without support from the most powerful military in the world for hours upon hours. With deleted emails and evasive answers at investigative hearings we may never know why. One thing I am confident of is - if Donald Trump was president at the time, help would have arrived sooner than it did. The root cause of these deaths was the wildly celebrated Arab Spring. Libya fell into chaos and their stockpile of sophistical weapons fell into the hands of terrorists. We had people there trying to destroy those weapons before they could be used on us. We also had diplomats there pretending everything was peaches and crème. The politically correct thing to do I guess.

Probably the major foreign policy "achievement" of the Obama administration is the Iran deal. We agreed to give them $150 billion and end economic sanctions against them. They agreed to let us know if they keep working on nuclear bombs. They are using these funds to build bombs, support terrorism and buy airplanes from Europe. They continue to pledge the total destruction of Israel, fund terrorism around the world and to destroy the American way of life. Only a miracle will prevent Iran from obtaining nuclear weapons under this agreement. Of course we don't know for sure because the American people don't know the details of the agreements. Only the people directly involved know their true motivations for agreeing to this deal. A nuclear Iran that is committed to the destruction of us and its neighbors will be the result of this deal. What exactly is our current administration committed to? Trump has made it clear that he is committed to our safety and I believe him. There is no need for a military button to be pushed if peaceful resolution is negotiated before it is too late.

It is not only our foreign policy actions that will have

negative implications for our future. It is our inaction as well. As our administrations have slept, China is building air force bases on atolls in the oil-rich South China Sea. They are claiming control over vast expanses of ocean used as the highways of ocean trade. They have ignored other countries' sovereign claims over these atolls. This has resulted in much friction among the countries involved. Once China completes its control over these vast areas of ocean it will be virtually impossible to peacefully reverse course. Not our business you might say. A student of history would say - not so fast. It was only 70 years ago we were attacked by Japan as part of their effort to conquer the entire western pacific. Japan's actions cost us dearly in American lives and treasure.

Trump has spoken out forcefully about China. He feels that we have let China dominate us in trade. He considers them smart and feels they aggressively take advantage of our "stupid" leaders. He is correct. They are doing what is good for them, not us. Who can blame them. Trump understands that China is primarily dependent on trade with America for its growing economy and thereby its domestic tranquility. We have allowed China to enjoy an "anything goes" relationship with us. They can dump their products on us while keeping their markets closed to our goods. They can pirate our brands and ignore our laws. They can build islands out of atolls in disputed territories for military bases. Trump fully understands that their economic dependence on us would allow peaceful negotiations regarding the South China Seas issue.

North Korea launched a long range missile around

the time of the New Hampshire Republican debate. The candidates were asked if they would preemptively destroy North Korean missiles before they could carry out nuclear attacks. All the candidates, except Trump, talked at length about what military action we should or should not take. They stayed on point as if military action by us was the only solution. Trump's answer was the clearest indication I have seen that he understands the world better than any of them. That he thinks differently. He correctly stated that North Korea was basically controlled by the Chinese. He said that we should pressure China to put an end to the nuclear threat from the North Koreans.

Trump didn't need rooms full of policy wonks to explain to him the realities of the world we live in. North Korea is dependent on China for their very survival. China's economy is dependent on American trade. Demand that China solve the problem. Keep our finger away from the button! Clear, knowledgeable, realistic thinking on his part. As an aside, North Korea got to this point in developing nuclear weapons because of the Clinton administration. In a deal eerily similar to the Iran deal, we paid them not to develop nuclear weapons. Like with Iran, we were to trust them. One does not need to be a fortune teller to see where we will be with Iran in a few years.

Russia has become much more active in world affairs of late. They have a very weak economy therefore their impact on the world is not as great as it once was. Our relationship with them is still of great importance. They recently said our relationship with them has regressed back to the

1962 level of animosity. Trump has been ridiculed for stating that he will work with them. I will just make one quick point about the current situation. Our last Secretary of State, Hillary Clinton, famously pushed the "reset button" during a photo opportunity while in Russia. It was a foolish, childish display of monumental proportions that ignored reality for the sake of a photo opportunity. The Russian leadership probably spilled their vodka that evening while toasting our incompetence. I have great confidence that a Trump administration would not make themselves the fool in this manner.

Trump has built a business empire thinking in terms of lifetimes. His children are now running the business. He has experience planning and acting for the long run. Our corrupt political system has our professional politicians thinking in 2, 4 or 6-year election cycles with very little concern beyond that. The world doesn't work that way. The Chinese and Muslims think and act in terms of centuries. As a businessperson he succeeds by anticipating events rather than constantly reacting to them. He has thought long-term rather than in election cycles. When conditions change, a businessperson changes with them. They don't blindly make decisions based on election promises. Trump has been mocked by the media for not ripping off a list of experienced foreign policy advisers he will rely upon, if elected. Personally, I think we would be better served by unbiased history teachers than the "experts" that have gotten us into this foreign policy mess. Trump would be more likely to keep our finger off the button than on it. And that sounds like a good thing to me.

Will A President Trump Make a Difference?

"If you don't see yourself as a winner, then you cannot perform as a winner."

Zig Ziglar

Since I wrote the book, **Trump: America Loves A Winner** I have been asked many times if I believe Trump could really make a difference. The answer is quite simple. He already has. Before he was even the republican nominee he has caused changes in our country. He has brought attention to issues that have been festering below the surface. Trump has sparked national conversations on government policies that have been harmful to our citizens. In many cases, people have been afraid to speak out for fear of being slandered and shouted down.

The following are a few examples of the impact Trump has already had on issues he talks about. Trump started talking about how we are paying for most of the cost of NATO and was quickly reamed in the press and by his opponents. Almost immediately thereafter, many foreign policy "experts" came out and said he was right. Now people are questioning why we are paying the costs to defend other countries. Our government has stood by and allowed corporations to do corporate inversions, which allows them to move jobs out of the country and reduce their tax bills. Trump continually mentioned Pfizer as an example, suddenly the Treasury Department changed their policy. Pfizer then cancelled their planned inversion. Trump has hammered the proposed TPP as a job killer similar to NAFTA. Now, the rush to enact the TPP agreement has slowed to a crawl. Even Hillary is changing her position of strongly supporting TPP when she was Secretary of State.

Trump has brought millions of disillusioned citizens to the primary voting booths. He has secured more votes in the republican primary than any candidate in history. He has already caused people who had given up on voting to give it one more shot. People throughout the country are beginning to discuss issues such as; a wall, campus speech and corruption in the election process, that had previously been taboo.

He has issued a list of potential Supreme Court Justice nominees. By doing so he has drawn a line in the sand for politicians. Any republican that wants to approve Obama's nominee will be telling the American people that they favor fewer rights for Americans. Hillary will ultimately be forced to come clean with us on what type of justice she will nominate. It was a masterstroke of genius on Trump's part that will haunt all future presidential candidates. They will be forced, in advance, to tell voters what they plan to do about our rights.

Trump has stood up to the dishonest media. He has put them on notice that their lies and misrepresentations will not be tolerated. The biased press will no longer be able to push false liberal and establishment narratives without being called out.

Our government is currently drastically reducing our military capabilities. We spent $1 billion on worthless Russian jets for Afghanistan while our air force scrounges for spare parts. As our military is being systematically dismantled, we are being put in harm's way from those who wish us ill. This is happening with a democrat president and a republican congress. Trump has unequivocally stated that he supports a strong military. He has spoken out strongly that our veterans deserve to be treated better and that he would insist that we do so. He has said he will put our safety first in the battle against terrorism and the invasion of illegal immigrants. Trump is also supportive of our police, once again indicating that he puts our safety as a priority.

Trump has stated he will put our economic interests first. He has said he would stop trade deals that ship our jobs to countries like China and Mexico. We spend billions defending South Korea while, as he has stated, buying their TVs due to unfair trade deals. He will stop the spending of billions and billions of dollars to support people that enter our country illegally. Trump is a successful and experienced international businessman. He knows how the financial system works. He will put our unbelievably talented Wall Street firms to work creating American jobs through sane government policies.

Trump is a pragmatic, cost-conscience leader. He understands that there are always costs for government actions. A businessperson like Trump has worked under the constraint of only spending what you can afford to spend. We have become a country that is becoming crippled because we spend as much as everyone wants to spend by borrowing. Hundreds of billions of dollars we spend are being wasted or stolen by fraud. Any of dozens of American companies could rapidly design systems to eliminate the billions of waste and fraud in programs such as Medicare and Obamacare. Trump would do just that. He would root out waste and fraud like a hog rooting out truffles.

Trump will have no incentive to strip away our rights and freedoms. Behind every freedom we lose are professional politicians and special interests with something to gain. Votes and money flow from dividing us. He will owe no favors to those that wish to strip away our freedoms. Although he says some unkind things about politicians and the media, Trump does not campaign by attempting to divide our citizens.

What is happening in our inner cities is a disgrace. Millions of people are living in crime-infested, burned out neighborhoods with not a job in sight. The very politicians claiming to represent them have created an inequality of life, in addition to an inequality of income. All the while, the professional politicians that claim to represent them waste money that could be used to help them. They hang out with Hollywood celebrities, take luxurious family trips around the world and play golf. Trump isn't running for president to do these things. He can do that now, with his own money. He is running to improve the lives of all Americans.

America loves a winner. Trump is a winner with a big personality and a bigger presence. He has not been run over by the media or the politicians that try to shout him down or to smear him. If elected, he will have the tenacity and winning persona to accomplish much of what he has said he will do. More importantly, he may provide inspiration to other politicians that have been afraid to buck the system. He has the potential to help elect a new breed of office holder that will actually do the will of the people.

This election may be the last chance to avoid irreparable damage to our future. The greatest imminent danger is the voting control by politicians that benefit from people paid not to work. These politicians have been busy getting more and more people dependent on government aid programs. They have greatly expanded the voter base that have no option but to vote for someone who continues to keep the work-free lifestyle as part of government policy. They are establishing a permanent underclass voter base of non-English speaking immigrants (legal and illegal). We are rapidly approaching the point where people who live off the government outnumber those who don't. We also have a weak job market and economy. And we are incurring an ever increasing national debt.

If you like the mess we are in, you have a member of a political Royal family to vote for. She has more baggage than a porter on the Orient Express. She knows how to spend your money. She has 10 times more campaign staff members for every one of Trumps, just to stay even with him. If you want at least a shot at righting our sinking ship, **Trump is your man**.

About the Author:
Ken Julien is a retired business executive turned author. He is a CPA and MBA. Born into a working class family he has been a member of six unions including the UAW. Ken resides in Arizona with his wife and two sons.

Ken Julien is the author of - Trump: America Loves A Winner

Copyright